# American Inside Out Evolution

Student's Book

Elementary

SUE KAY
VAUGHAN JONES

macmillan education

# Contents

# Walkthrough

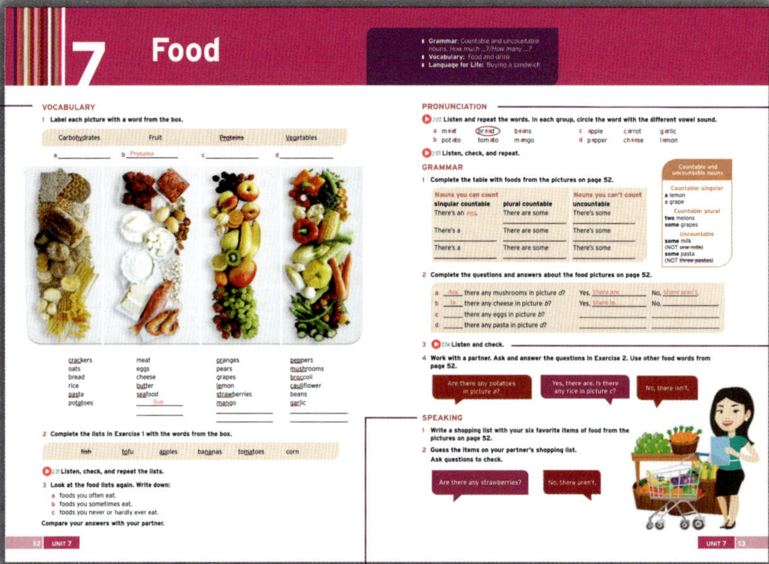


## VOCABULARY

- Vocabulary is presented in a meaningful context and is related to the topics in the unit.
- Clear pictures help acquisition.
- There are practice activities to expand your knowledge of particular lexical sets and give you opportunities to use the new vocabulary in social exchanges.
- You will also listen to the words and repeat them before manipulating them in real social contexts.

## PRONUNCIATION

Pronunciation work on particular areas of sound, stress, and intonation is integrated into every unit.

## LISTENING

The listening activities include texts specially written for language learning - dialogues, conversations, and monologues. They were carefully designed to develop real life listening skills.

## SPEAKING

You will have plenty of opportunities to speak throughout the unit using language learned.

## READING

Contemporary reading texts have been adapted and graded to suit each level. They have been selected not only for their language content but also for their interest and appropriacy. The texts are supported by recordings.

## GRAMMAR

- Here you will explore new grammatical structures that have been contextualized in the reading / listening sections. You will focus on the way language works.
- A brief summary of the grammar point is provided in the margin.
- Language is explored in realistic and meaningful practice exercises.
- You will use target language in controlled and personalized practice.

## WRITING

Motivating writing practice is provided in a task where you will follow a model. The writing activities are also based on varied texts that you write on everyday life. There is also a comprehensive writing course in the Workbook.

The Grammar Extra pages at the back of the Student's Book extend explanations and provide further practice.

## LANGUAGE FOR LIFE

The Language for Life section gives you a portable toolkit of functional language. Here, you notice how language is more than just form. You will see language in fun, engaging social situations.

## VOCABULARY EXTRA

The Vocabulary Extra pages at the end of every unit recycle the key vocabulary items taught in the unit. This provides an activated wordlist and a useful bank of vocabulary.

## LIFE SKILLS

Developing life skills alongside language skills is an essential requirement to meet the demands of the contemporary world.

*American Inside Out Evolution* has a Life Skills section in every unit. Life Skills present activities in order for you to reflect on and discuss the skills you need for social and work situations in today's world.

## REVIEW

There are Review units in the Student's Book. They review the new structures and vocabulary taught in the previous teaching units.

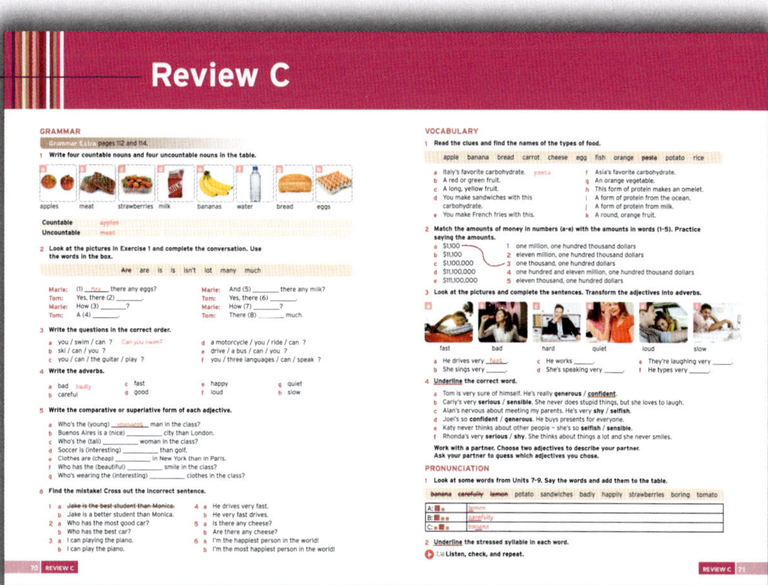

There is one Pairwork activity for every unit, which offers further speaking practice.

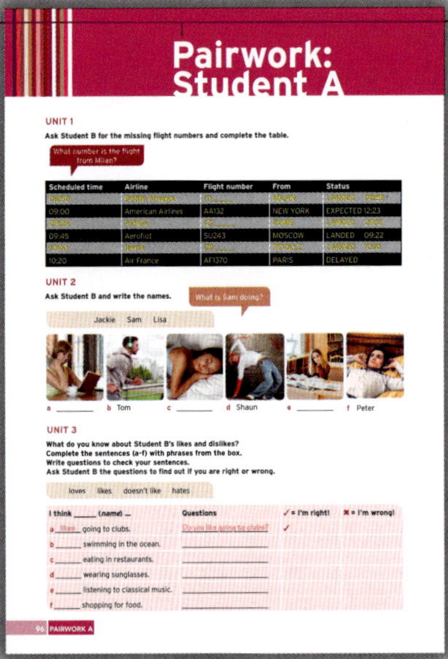


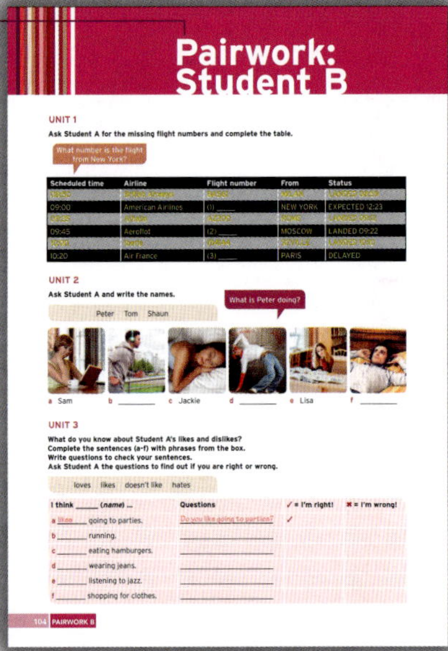


**GRAMMAR EXTRA**

The Grammar Extra pages at the back of the Student's Book provide a summary of the new grammatical structures, as well as extra practice.

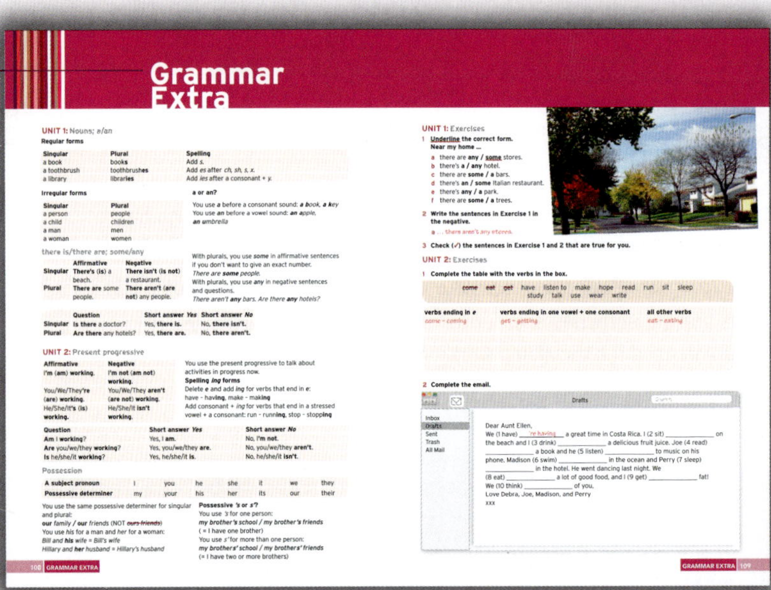


The Workbook provides a review of all the main points in the Student's Book, plus extra listening practice, pronunciation work, and a writing program.

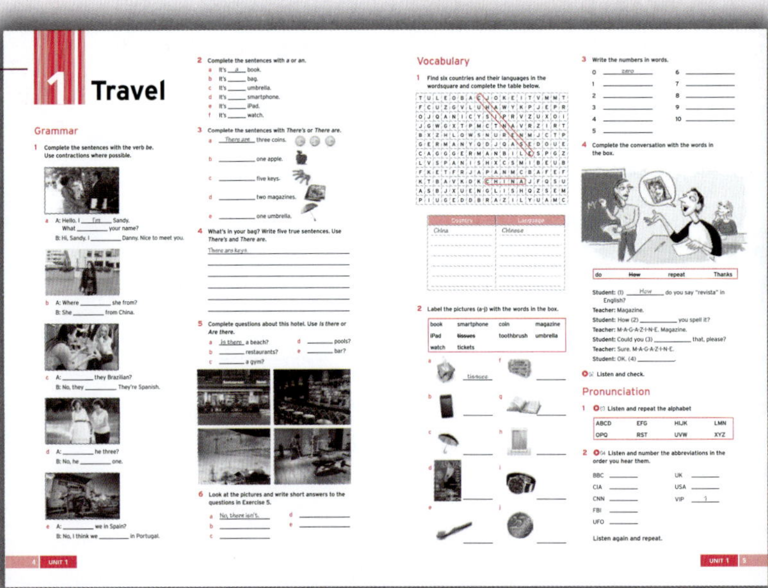

# Student's Components

Student's Book with access code to Digital Student's Book

Workbook with access code to Digital Workbook

# 1 Travel

## LISTENING & SPEAKING

1 1.02 **Read and listen to the conversation. Answer the questions.**

a What's his name?
b What's her name?
c Where's she from?

A: Hi. I'm Mike. What's your name?
B: Oh, hello. I'm Julia.
A: Nice to meet you. Are you American?
B: No, I'm not. I'm Brazilian. I'm from Rio de Janeiro.

**Listen and repeat.**

2 **Introduce yourself to people in the class.**

Hi. I'm Rosa. What's your name?

I'm Jon.

Nice to meet you. Where are you from?

I'm from Madrid.

## VOCABULARY

1 1.03 **Listen and repeat the country and nationality. Underline the stressed syllables.**

| Country | Nationality | Language |
|---|---|---|
| *I'm from ...* | *I'm ...* | *I speak ...* |
| Brazil | Brazilian | (1) Portuguese |
| Germany | German | (2) German |
| Italy | Italian | (3) ________ |
| Mexico | Mexican | (4) ________ |
| Australia | Australian | (5) ________ |
| Spain | Spanish | (6) ________ |
| China | Chinese | (7) ________ |
| Japan | Japanese | (8) ________ |

2 1.04 **Listen and complete the languages.**

3 **Say a country. Your partner says the nationality and the language.**

Brazil?

Brazilian, Portuguese

- **Grammar:** *be:* simple present. *a/an. there is/are*
- **Vocabulary:** Countries. Nationalities. Numbers 0-10. Objects. The alphabet.
- **Language for Life:** Asking for clarification

## GRAMMAR

**1 Complete the questions and answers.**

a __Is__ he Chinese? Yes, __he is__. No, __he isn't__.
b ________ they Spanish? Yes, ________. No, ________.
c ________ it Japanese? Yes, ________. No, ________.
d ________ she Mexican? Yes, ________. No, ________.
e ________ it German? Yes, ________. No, ________.
f ________ they British? Yes, ________. No, ________.

1.05 **Listen, check, and repeat.**

**2 Ask questions about the pictures.**

a

b

c

d

e

f

g

Is it German?

No, it isn't. It's British.

## PRONUNCIATION

1 1.06 **Listen and repeat the vowels A, E, I, O, U.**

2 1.07 **Listen and repeat the consonants and vowels.**

3 1.08 **Listen and write the order in which you hear these groups of vowels.**

a A E I O U ☐
b A I O E U ☐
c E I A U O [1]
d I A O U E ☐
e I U A O E ☐

## VOCABULARY

1 1.09 **Listen and repeat the numbers.**

2 1.10 **Listen and complete the telephone numbers for these airlines.**

a

LATAM: 1-866-435-9526

b

American Airlines: 800-433-_____

c

British Airways: 0344-493- _____

d

Air Canada: 1-_____-393-3333

e

TAP: 1-__-____-70

f

United Airlines: 1-800-864-_____

3 **Pairwork Student A:** page 96 **Student B:** page 100

### *be*

| | |
|---|---|
| I**'m** | I **am** |
| You**'re** | You **are** |
| He**'s** | He **is** |
| She**'s** | She **is** |
| It**'s** | It **is** |
| We**'re** | We **are** |
| They**'re** | They **are** |

**Is** he Spanish?
Yes, he **is**.
No, he **isn't**.

**Are** they American?
Yes, they **are**.
No, they **aren't**.

### The alphabet

| Sounds | Letters |
|---|---|
| /eɪ/ | A H J K |
| /i/ | B C D E G P T V Z |
| /e/ | F L M N S X |
| /aɪ/ | I Y |
| /oʊ/ | O |
| /u/ | Q U W |
| /ɑ/ | R |

### Numbers

0 = zero / oh
1 = one 6 = six
2 = two 7 = seven
3 = three 8 = eight
4 = four 9 = nine
5 = five 10 = ten

212-634-5789 =
two one two
six three four
five seven eight nine

## VOCABULARY & LISTENING

**1** 1.11 **Listen and repeat the words.**

**2** 1.12 **Read and listen to the conversations. Which is Mike's bag? Which is Julia's bag?**

1 **Customs:** OK. What's in your bag, sir?
**Mike:** Oh, a toothbrush, a magazine ...
**Customs:** And what's this, sir?
**Mike:** It's an iPad.
**Customs:** Hm. What are these?
**Mike:** They're tickets.

2 **Customs:** What's in your bag, ma'am?
**Julia:** An umbrella, a book ...
**Customs:** And what's this?
**Julia:** It's a smartphone.
**Customs:** And what are these?
**Julia:** They're headphones.

**3** **Work with a partner. Practice the conversations.**

## GRAMMAR

**1** **Complete the table.**

| **Singular** | **Plural** |
|---|---|
| a magazine | (1) magazines |
| (2) ____________ | iPads |
| (3) ____________ | umbrellas |
| (4) ____________ | pens |

1.13 **Listen, check, and repeat.**

**2** **Look at the pictures (a-f). Write questions and answers with *this/it* and *these/they*.**

a What's this? It's a book.

a 
a book

b 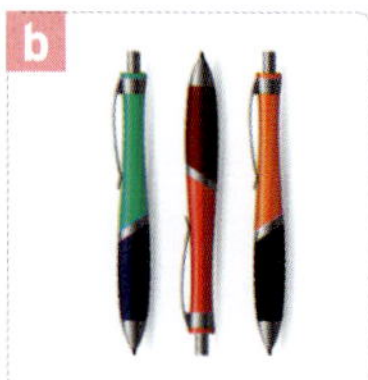
pens

c 
keys

d 
coins

e 
a bag

f 
watches

1.14 **Listen, check, and repeat.**

### Nouns

**Singular**

What's **this**?
It's **a** book.
It's **an** umbrella.

consonant sound =
**a** (**a** pen)
vowel sound =
**an** (**an** iPad)

**Plural**

What are **these**?
They're **books**.

## VOCABULARY & READING

**1 Look at the pictures and label the photos.**

pool ~~hotel~~ room beach bar restaurant

thebeachhouse.com

# The Beach House

**a** hotel

Welcome to paradise! **The Beach House** is your perfect vacation hotel.

There are many luxury rooms and suites. The view is wonderful. There are three restaurants at our hotel. There's a beach bar for a relaxing drink. There are two pools — indoor and outdoor — and a gym. And of course, there's our perfect beach. Check in to **The Beach House** today!

**b** ____________

**c** ____________

**d** ____________

**e** ____________

**f** ____________

1.15 **Listen, check, and repeat.**

**2 Read the text. Are the sentences true (T) or false (F)?**

- **a** There are three pools. [F]
- **b** There are two restaurants. [ ]
- **c** There's a beach. [ ]
- **d** There are many rooms. [ ]
- **e** There's a gym. [ ]

1.16 **Listen and check.**

**3 Would you like to stay at this hotel? Tell your partner.**

## GRAMMAR

**1 Complete the questions and answers about the hotel.**

- **a** __Is__ there a beach? Yes, __there is.__ No, __there isn't.__
- **b** __Are__ there any rooms? Yes, __there are.__ No, ________.
- **c** ________ there ________ pool? ________. ________.
- **d** ________ there ________ restaurants? ________. ________.
- **e** ________ there ________ bar? ________. ________.

1.17 **Listen, check, and repeat.**

**2 Think about a hotel you have visited. Work with a partner. Ask and answer the questions in Exercise 1.**

**3** **Grammar Extra 1** page 104. Read the explanation and do the exercises.

### *there is/there are, some/any*

**Singular**

**There's** a beach.
**There isn't** a bar.

**Is there** a pool?
Yes, **there is**.
No, **there isn't**.

**Plural**

In the plural, use **some** with positive sentences and **any** with negative sentences.
**There are some** people.
**There aren't any** restaurants.

**Are there any** rooms?
Yes, **there are**.
No, **there aren't**.

## LANGUAGE FOR LIFE

**1** 1.18 **Read, listen, and complete the conversation with *say, spell*, or *repeat*.**

**Student:** How do you (1) ___say___ "Francia" in English?
**Teacher:** "France".
**Student:** How do you (2) ____________ it?
**Teacher:** F-R-A-N-C-E.
**Student:** Ah, yes. "France." How do you (3) ____________ "Itália" in English?
**Teacher:** "Italy."
**Student:** How do you (4) ____________ it?
**Teacher:** I-T-A-L-Y.
**Student:** Oh, yes. "Italy." English is easy. How do you (5) ____________ "Alemania"?
**Teacher:** "Germany."
**Student:** Excuse me?
**Teacher:** "Germany."
**Student:** How do you (6) ____________ it?
**Teacher:** G-E-R-M-A-N-Y.
**Student:** Can you (7) ____________ that, please?
**Teacher:** G-E-R-M-A-N-Y.
**Student:** OK, thanks.

**2** 1.19 **Listen and repeat the expressions.**

a How do you say "Francia" in English?
b How do you spell it?
c Excuse me?
d Can you repeat that, please?
e OK, thanks.

**3 Practice the conversation.**

### Life Skills: Social Skills
Giving & receiving feedback

**1** 1.20 **Listen and complete the conversations using the words in the box.**

| ~~right~~ again done try not |
|---|

a **STUDENT:** Is the answer "Italy"?
**TEACHER:** Yes, that's (1) ___right___. Well (2) ________.
**STUDENT:** Thank you.

b **STUDENT:** Is the answer "Spain"?
**TEACHER:** No, it's (3) ________. Please look at the question (4) ________.
**STUDENT:** Ah, is the answer "Spanish"?

c **STUDENT:** I don't know how to write it.
**TEACHER:** Please (5) ________.
**STUDENT:** OK.

**2 Do you think this feedback is positive or negative? Draw a happy 🙂 or sad ☹ emoji.**

| | |
|---|---|
| That's wrong. | No, sorry. |
| Great job. | Good work. |
| Fantastic. | Not good enough. |

**3 Practice giving feedback to your partner.**

I got the answer right!

Good job, Paula!

MACMILLAN LIFE SKILLS

# 1 Vocabulary Extra

## Common nouns

1 **Match the pictures with the words.**

| Singular | | Plural |
|---|---|---|
| __1__ | a bag | ______ |
| ______ | a ______ | books |
| ______ | a smartphone | ______ |
| ______ | a coin | ______ |
| ______ | a ______ | keys |
| ______ | a magazine | ______ |
| ______ | an iPad | ______ |
| ______ | a ticket | ______ |
| ______ | a ______ | tissues |
| ______ | a toothbrush | ______ |
| ______ | an umbrella | ______ |
| ______ | a ______ | watches |
| ______ | a pen | ______ |

2 **Complete the singular or plural forms in Exercise 1.**

3 **Work with a partner. Cover the words and look at the pictures. Ask and answer questions.**

What's this? It's a bag. What are these? They're keys.

## Focus on instructions

1 **Match the pictures with the phrases.**

__3__ Listen to the conversation.
______ Look at the board.
______ Read the text.
______ Work with a partner.
______ Write your name on a piece of paper.
______ Use a dictionary.

2 **Complete the instructions with verbs from Exercise 1.**

a __Read__ the article.
b ______ at the picture on page 9.
c ______ the answer on a piece of paper.
d ______ to the song.
e ______ in groups of three.
f ______ the answers to the questions.

# 2 People

## READING & VOCABULARY

**1 Complete the posts about Zara's family. Use the words in the box.**

| ~~brother~~ | brother | sister | parents | cousins | friend | son | daughter | aunt |
|---|---|---|---|---|---|---|---|---|

zara101

**a** This is me and my brother, Zach. He's so great.

zara101

**b** My older _______, Louise, getting married to my new _______-in-law, Andy. What a day!

zara101

**c** My lovely _______. Smile, mom and dad!

zara101

**d** My uncle Tony and my _______ Jean with my cousins Tom, and Sally.

zara101

**e** My best _______, Carey, with her _______, Tim, and her _______, Amy. Hi, guys!

zara101

**f** Two of my favorite _______, Frank and Nina!

1.21 **Listen and check.**

## GRAMMAR

**1 Complete the sentences with *my*, *your*, *his*, *her*, *its*, *our* or *their*.**

**a** I'm a singer. ___My___ sister is Solange Knowles.
**b** He's from Springfield, in the USA. _____________ son's name is Bart.
**c** She's from Britain. _____________ albums include *21* and *25*.
**d** We're married. _____________ names are Kanye and Kim.
**e** They're American. _____________ last name is Clinton.

1.22 **Listen and check.**

**2 Work with a partner. Who are the people in Exercise 1?**

| Subject pronoun | Possessive determiner |
|---|---|
| I | my |
| you | your |
| he | his |
| she | her |
| it | its |
| we | our |
| they | their |

## GRAMMAR

**1 Who says it? Look again at Zara's family. Match the sentences with the names.**

**a** My husband's name is Tony. — Andy
**b** My cousins' names are Frank and Nina. — Zach
**c** My wife's name is Louise. — Jean
**d** My sister's name is Zara. — Zara
**e** My best friend's name is Zara. — Carey

**Possessive *'s/s'***

Her father**'s** name is Peter. (*father* is singular)

Her brother**s'** names are Tom and Jack. (*brothers* is plural)

- **Grammar:** Possessive determiners, *'s/s'*. Simple present. Present progressive
- **Vocabulary:** Family. Jobs. Clothes. Numbers *11-999*.
- **Language for Life:** Imperatives

## VOCABULARY

**Numbers**

11 = eleven
12 = twelve
13 = thirteen
14 = fourteen
15 = fifteen
16 = sixteen
17 = seventeen
18 = eighteen
19 = nineteen

20 = twenty
30 = thirty
40 = forty
50 = fifty
60 = sixty
70 = seventy
80 = eighty
90 = ninety
100 = one hundred
200 = two hundred

1 1.23 **Listen and repeat the numbers.**

2 1.24 **Listen and circle the numbers you hear. Repeat the numbers.**

a (13) / 30  b 14 / 40  c 15 / 50  d 16 / 60  e 17 / 70

3 **Write the numbers in numerals.**

a thirteen 13
b twenty-eight ______
c sixty-five ______
d one hundred and ten ______

1.25 **Listen and repeat.**

## SPEAKING

1 **Match an age from the box with a person below. Discuss with a partner.**

52 19 82 9 41 5 64 23 29

a 
b 
c 
d 

2 **Write the ages in words.**

a She's ______. b ______. c ______. d ______.

1.26 **Listen and check your ideas.**

## VOCABULARY

1 **Match the jobs with the pictures.**

a dentist  a doctor  a hairdresser  a police officer
a lawyer  a taxi driver  nurses  sales clerks

a 
b 
c 
d 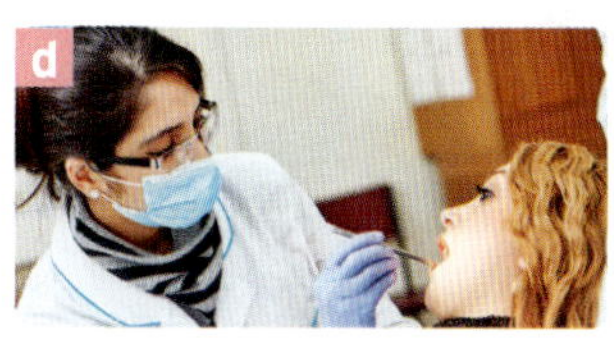
e 
f 
g 
h 

**Write sentences.**

a She's a police officer. b He's a hairdresser. c They're sales clerks. d ______.
e ______. f ______. g ______. h ______.

1.27 **Listen, check, and repeat.**

2 1.28 **Work with a partner. Listen to the information about the percentage (%) of women in different jobs in the USA. Match the jobs and percentages.**

91% ~~23%~~ 13% 28% 6% 35% 93% 51%

a dentists 23%
b doctors ______
c nurses ______
d police officers ______
e lawyers ______
f hairdressers ______
g sales clerks ______
h taxi drivers ______

**Listen again and check.**

## VOCABULARY

**1 Look at the website for The Clothing Company. Check (✓) the items you can see in the picture.**

**The Clothing Company.**

Home | About | Shop | Contact

All Clothing | Men's | Women's | Kids' | Brands | Sale | New | search

**footwear**

boots
shoes ✓
sneakers

**casual clothes**

jeans
sweaters
tops
sweatpants
T-shirts

**formal clothes**

overcoats
jackets
shirts
suits
skirts
ties
pants
dresses

**accessories**

bags
belts
hats
rings
sunglasses

1.29 **Listen and repeat all the words.**

**2 Complete the following table with clothes and accessories from Exercise 1.**

| A: Singular nouns (a ...) | B: Plural nouns (a pair of ...) |
|---|---|
| an overcoat, a jacket | a pair of boots, a pair of shoes |

1.30 **Listen, check, and repeat.**

## PRONUNCIATION

**1** 1.31 **Listen and repeat the chants.**

**A**
jeans and jackets
belts and boots
casual clothes
casual clothes

**B**
shoes and socks
shirts and suits
formal clothes
formal clothes

**2 Complete the table with the plural nouns in the chant.**

| Plural nouns ending in /s/ | Plural nouns ending in /z/ |
|---|---|
| jackets, | jeans, |

## LISTENING

**1** 1.32 **Listen to an interview with The Clothing Company customers. Underline the correct answer.**

a She's a **nurse** / **lawyer**. She's looking for **shoes** / **a skirt**.
b He's a **taxi driver** / **sales clerk**. He's looking for **sneakers** / **boots**.
c She's a **hairdresser** / **police officer**. She's looking for **sunglasses** / **belts**.
d He's a **teacher** / **doctor**. He's looking for **a suit** / **pants**.

**2 Listen again. How much do they want to spend?**

a $ 50 b $____ c $____ d $____

## GRAMMAR

1 **Complete the questions and answers with a pronoun and the correct form of *be*.**

a __Are__ you wearing jeans? Yes, __I am__. No, __I'm not__.
b ______ you sitting next to a window? Yes, ______. No, ______.
c ______ your teacher standing up? Yes, ______. No, ______.
d ______ the traffic making a noise? Yes, ______. No, ______.
e ______ all of you wearing a watch? Yes, ______. No, ______.
f ______ the birds singing outside? Yes, ______. No, ______.

1.33 **Listen, check, and repeat.**

2 **Work with a partner. Ask and answer the questions in Exercise 1.**

3 **Think of three people in your family. Guess what they are doing right now. Tell your partner.**

I think my father is working. My sister is doing her homework, and my brother is playing the guitar.

4 **Grammar Extra 2** page 104. Read the explanation and do the exercises.

5 **Pairwork Student A:** page 96. **Student B:** page 100

**Present progressive**

I**'m**
You**'re**
He**'s**
She**'s** **working**.
It**'s**
We**'re**
They**'re**

**Are** you **working**?
Yes, I **am**.
No, I**'m not**.

**Is** she **working**?
Yes, she **is**.
No, she **isn't**.

## LISTENING

1 1.34 **Listen to the radio presenter, Ross White, describing people as they arrive for the Oscars. Put the pictures (a-c) in the correct order (1-3).**

a

b

c

2 **Match the verb phrases in column A with the phrases in column B.**

| | A | B |
|---|---|---|
| a | I'm waiting for | around. |
| b | She's wearing | at everyone. |
| c | She's turning | a beautiful dress. |
| d | He's wearing | the big stars. |
| e | He's smiling | a black suit. |

1.35 **Listen and check. Who is doing each action?**

## LANGUAGE FOR LIFE

**1 Complete the expressions (a-d) with the verbs in the box.**

| be | Call | ~~Drive~~ | Have | Smile | worry |
|---|---|---|---|---|---|

a 

b 

c 

d 

a ___Drive___ carefully. Don't ________ late.

b ________! Say cheese!

c Don't ________! He's OK.

d ________ a good time. Take care. ________ me.

1.36 **Listen, check, and repeat.**

**2 Read the conversation. Cross out *Don't* where necessary.**

**Lauren:** Bye, Mom. Bye, Dad.
**Dad:** (1) ~~Don't~~ **drive carefully.**
**Lauren:** (2) **Don't worry,** Dad.
**Mom:** (3) **Don't have a good time** in New York.
**Lauren:** Thanks, Mom.
**Dad:** (4) **Don't forget** your phone.
**Lauren:** OK. My phone's in my bag.
**Mom:** (5) **Don't call us.** (6) **Don't take care.**
**Lauren:** OK. Bye. See you!

1.37 **Listen, check, and repeat.**

**Work in groups of three.**
**Practice the conversation.**

### Life Skills: Analyzing Information
Job Applications

**1** 1.38 **Listen and complete the job application.**

**2 Work with a partner and answer the questions.**

a Who is she?
b What is her experience?
c What are her skills?

**Job Application**

**Name** *
(1) Rosie | Gray
First | Last

**Job:**
(2) ________________

**Experience**:
(3) ______ years at Brilliant English Academy, Beijing, China
(4) ______ years at Oxford School of English, São Paulo, Brazil
1 year teacher training at ELF Institute, London, the UK

**About**:
- smart and organized
- good with (5) ________________
- strong leader

**3 Look at the two applications for a job as a nurse. Who is your favorite candidate? Why?**

**Job Application**

**Name** *
Mike | Mills
First | Last

**Job:**
nurse

**Experience**
- 3 years as Senior Nurse at Franklin Hospital
- 3 years as Nurse at Windle Valley Clinic

**About**:
- good energy
- friendly

**Job Application**

**Name** *
Freda | McDonald
First | Last

**Job:**
nurse

**Experience**
- 12 years as Nurse at St. Mary's Hospital
- 1 year as Nursing Assistant at Westchester Care Home

**About**:
- fun
- speaks 3 languages

MACMILLAN LIFE SKILLS

# 2 Vocabulary Extra

## Clothes

**1 Match the pictures with the words.**

| | | | |
|---|---|---|---|
| __6__ a belt | ______ an overcoat | ______ sneakers | ______ sweatpants |
| ______ boots | ______ pants | ______ socks | ______ a top |
| ______ a hat | ______ a shirt | ______ a skirt | ______ a T-shirt |
| ______ a jacket | ______ shoes | ______ a suit | |

**2 Work with a partner. Cover the words and look at the pictures. Ask and answer questions.**

What's this?

It's a jacket.

What are these?

They're boots.

## Focus on numbers

**1 Write the numbers.**

| 11 = eleven | 20 = twenty | 121 = one hundred and twenty-one |
|---|---|---|
| 12 = | 30 = | 257 = |
| 13 = | 40 = | 376 = |
| 14 = | 50 = | 492 = |
| 15 = | 60 = | 533 = |
| 16 = | 70 = | 648 = |
| 17 = | 80 = | 764 = |
| 18 = | 90 = | 805 = |
| 19 = | 100 = | 999 = |

**2 Dictate any three numbers from 1 to 999 to your partner.**

54

736

989

fifty-four

seven hundred and thirty-six

nine hundred and eighty-nine

# 3 Likes

## READING

**1 Read and complete. Use *He* or *She* according to your own ideas.**

**At the mall ...**

1 __She__ goes to the mall just to hang out.
2 _____ buys only one thing and leaves.
3 _____ visits many stores to compare prices.

**At the airport ...**

1 _____ checks in two hours early.
2 _____ does some shopping before boarding.
3 _____ sits and watches TV at the gate.

**At the restaurant ...**

1 _____ orders a salad.
2 _____ orders a dessert.
3 _____ has a beer.

**Online**

1 _____ checks out the latest celebrity news.
2 _____ checks the sports scores.
3 _____ watches funny cat videos.

**2 Compare your answers with a partner. Which answers are different?**

**3 Think about your own experience.**

a Check (✓) the action in the text that you do.
b Put a cross (✖) next to the action that you don't do.

- **Grammar:** Simple present. Object pronouns.
- **Vocabulary:** *like/don't like + ing*
- **Language for Life:** Opinions

## READING & LISTENING

1 **Complete the opinions of the people below using the words in the box.**

~~sneakers~~ online sports cars fast shoe

# We're Different!

a 
**sneakerboy · 3h**
I love (1) sneakers . I have about ten pairs and I'm looking for more. I like to enter (2) ________ stores to look at them. My wife hates shoe store. She only has one pair of sneakers!
like · reply · share

b 
**yankeesfan99 · 5h**
I have to say sorry to my husband. Romantic dinner? I go online and check out the (3) ________ scores. I want to know about my team, the New York Yankees, all the time. My husband doesn't like sports. He just goes (4) ________ to watch funny cat videos!
like · reply · share

c 
**safeandgray · 7h**
We have two (5) ________. I drive a very normal car. It's a gray sedan. It's comfortable. My wife drives a new Ford Mustang. And she drives it very, very (6) ________. I don't go in her car very often.
like · reply · share

1.39 **Listen and check.**

2 **Underline the affirmative or negative form to make true sentences.**

a I **have / don't have** ten pairs of sneakers.
b I **go / don't go** online to check sports scores.
c I **watch / don't watch** funny videos online.
d I **drive / don't drive** a sports car.

**Compare your sentences with a partner.**

## GRAMMAR

1 **Complete the questions and answers.**

a Do you like shopping? Yes, I do. No, I don't.
b Does your father do the housework? Yes, he does. No, he doesn't.
c Do you think about chocolate all the time? Yes, ________. No, ________.
d ______ your mother work on weekends? ________. ________.
e ______ you and your friends chat online? ________. ________.

1.40 **Listen, check, and repeat.**

2 **Write true sentences about you from the prompts. Use affirmative or negative forms.**

a work / in a restaurant *I don't work in a restaurant.*
b sing / in the shower
c play / tennis
d speak /Spanish

3 **Ask your partner questions using the prompts in Exercise 2. Write the answers.**

Do you work in a restaurant?
No, I don't.
*She doesn't work in a restaurant.*

4 **Grammar Extra 3** page 106. Read the explanation and do the exercises.

**Simple present**

I / You / We / They **work**. / **don't work**.

**Do** you **work**?
Yes, I **do**.
No, I **don't**.

He / She / It **works**. / **doesn't work**.

**Does** he **work**?
Yes, he **does**.
No, he **doesn't**.

## VOCABULARY & LISTENING

**1 Complete using words and phrases from the box.**

don't like   don't mind   hate   like   ~~love~~   really like

I (1) __love__ it.   I (2) ______ it.   I (3) ______ it.   I (4) ______ it.   I (5) ______ it.   I (6) ______ it.

1.41 **Listen, check, and repeat.**

**2 Read about Phil and Kesha.**

**Phil, 35**

Phil loves the countryside. He really likes being outside, doing sports, and staying in shape. He hates cities and he doesn't like loud music.

**Kesha, 25**

Kesha loves spending money! She loves dancing and doesn't mind loud music. She hates cooking and doing housework, and doesn't like sports.

**3 Look at the activities in the box. Put P if you think Phil likes it. Put K if you think Kesha likes it.**

clubbing ☐   eating fast food ☐   cooking ☐   going to the gym ☐
playing soccer ☐   running ☐   going to the mall ☐   swimming ☐

1.42 **Listen and check your answers. Are you like Phil or Kesha?**

## SPEAKING

**1 Complete the table to show the spelling of the *ing* form.**

| Most verbs | Verbs ending in *e* | Verbs ending in vowel + consonant |
|---|---|---|
| read → __reading__ | dance → __dancing__ | swim → __swimming__ |
| walk → (1) ______ | smoke → (3) ______ | shop → (5) ______ |
| cook → (2) ______ | drive → (4) ______ | run → (6) ______ |

**2 Ask your partner questions. Use the verbs in Exercise 1.**

Do you like reading?

Yes, I do. / It's OK. / No, I don't.

**3 Pairwork Student A:** page 96   **Student B:** page 100

## PRONUNCIATION

1 **Complete the chants with *flying, talking,* or *thinking.***

**A**
Running, walking,
Listening, __________.

**B**
Eating, drinking,
Sleeping, __________.

**C**
Selling, buying,
Sailing, __________.

1.43 **Listen, check, and repeat.**

## GRAMMAR

1 **Complete the sentences with *him, her, it* or *them.***

**a** I don't like The Beatles. Do you like ___them___?
**b** I don't like Justin Bieber. Do you like __________?
**c** I don't like Taylor Swift. Do you like __________?
**d** I don't like Kanye West. Do you like __________?
**e** I don't like Maroon 5. Do you like __________?
**f** I don't like dance music. Do you like ______________?

**Pronouns**

| Subject | Object |
|---|---|
| I | me |
| you | you |
| he | him |
| she | her |
| it | it |
| we | us |
| they | them |

1.44 **Listen, check, and repeat.**

2 **Write a short blog post about people or things you don't like.**

blogging.com

**blogging.com** HOME PHOTOS BLOG

Publish New Post Save Close

I don't like classical music.
I don't like doing the dishes.

3 **Read your sentences and ask for your partner's opinion.**

I don't like classical music. Do you like it?

Yes, I do.

## READING & WRITING

1 **Read and complete the profile with an object pronoun from the box.**

~~me~~ me you him
her it it us them

1.45 **Listen and check.**

makingfriends.com

**making friends** HOME ABOUT PROFILES search

**Bianca, 24**
15 miles away
active 1 day ago

**About** (1) ___me___

My name's Bianca – and yes, that's (2) ________ in the picture!
I'm 24 and I'm a Libra. I'm single.
I work for a tech company. I'm a software developer. It's a good job, but I don't like (3) ________.
My favorite person in the world is my brother. I love (4) ________ but we're very different. He has a girlfriend, but my parents don't like (5) ________.
We live at home with our parents. We also have a sister, but she doesn't live with (6) ________. She has her own family and we only see her on the weekend.
I love music. I listen to hip-hop and jazz. I have piano lessons, but I can't play (7) ________ very well yet.
I like going to clubs and dancing. I have many friends and I go out with (8) ________ on a Friday night.
What about (9) ________?

2 **Write a similar social profile about you.**

**Analisa, 25**
My name's Analisa.
That's me in the picture.
I'm ...

**Compare your profile with a partner.**

## LANGUAGE FOR LIFE

**1** 1.46 **Read and listen to the conversations. Underline the adjectives you hear.**

**a** **Ann:** What do you think of Pharrell Williams?
**Bob:** I think he's **great / OK / terrible.**
**Ann:** I agree. I really like him.

**b** **Fran:** What do you think of Coldplay?
**Salvatore:** I think they're **great / OK / terrible**. What about you?
**Fran:** I don't agree. I think they're **great / OK / terrible**.

**c** **Cathy:** What do you think of Emma Watson?
**Debra:** I think she's **great / OK / terrible**. What about you?
**Cathy:** I think she's **great / OK / terrible**, but I prefer Jennifer Lawrence.

**d** **Harry:** What do you think of Neymar?
**Isobel:** Who?
**Harry:** Neymar. He's a soccer player.
**Isobel:** I don't know. What do you think of him?
**Harry:** I think he's **great / OK / terrible.**

**2** **Complete the table with the expressions from the conversation.**

~~What do you think of Pharrell Williams?~~ ~~I think he's great.~~ I think he's OK. I prefer Jennifer Lawrence. I think they're terrible. What about you? I don't know.

| Asking for an opinion | Giving an opinion |
|---|---|
| *What do you think of Pharrell Williams?* | *I think he's great.* |
| | |
| | |

1.47 **Listen, check, and repeat the expressions.**

**3** **Write a list of your favorite actors, singers, bands, and writers. Ask your partner's opinion about the people on the list.**

### Life Skills: Social Responsibility
Older Generations

**1** 1.48 **Read about three grandparents.**

**a Anna**

My name's Anna. I live alone in Detroit. It's lonely. My son and daughter live in California. I don't talk to them. I don't have a cell phone. I'd like to speak to my grandkids.

**b Luis**

Hi, I'm Luis. I live here in Los Angeles. I don't have a lot of money so it's difficult to buy food or medicine. My daughter sometimes gives me some money, but I don't like it. She has two daughters and needs the money, too.

**c Shen**

Hi, I'm Shen. I live in New York now to be near my family. I don't speak English very well. I don't really understand what my grandchildren are saying. Life in China is easier.

**2** **What does each grandparent need? Match each thing to a, b, or c.**

money ☐ medicine ☐ a cell phone ☐
English lessons ☐ a webcam ☐ friends ☐

**3** **Discuss your ideas with a partner.**

Shen needs English lessons.

MACMILLAN LIFE SKILLS

# 3 Vocabulary Extra

## Common verbs

**1 Match the pictures with the verbs. Then complete the verb phrases.**

| | | | | | |
|---|---|---|---|---|---|
| 5 | buy | a pair of shoes | ____ | smoke | ______ |
| ____ | drink | ______ | ____ | speak | ______ |
| ____ | drive | ______ | ____ | spend | ______ |
| ____ | eat | ______ | ____ | think | ______ |
| ____ | live | ______ | ____ | watch | ______ |
| ____ | play | ______ | ____ | work | ______ |

1

Spanish

2

TV

3

a car

4

a cigarette

5

a pair of shoes

6

about chocolate

7

beer

8

soccer

9

for a big company

10

in a big city

11

$50

12

fries

**2 Work with a partner. Cover the words and look at the pictures. Ask and answer questions.**

What is number 1?

Speak Spanish.

## Focus on instructions

**1 Complete the instructions with the verbs in the box.**

~~Check~~ Circle Complete
Cross out Match Underline

**1**
a He loves me.
b He loves me. ✓

**2**
I love her and
she loves me.

**3**
We love them
and they love us.

**4**
I — him
you — me
he — her
she — you

**5**
a I love her.
~~b I love she.~~

**6**
me you
him her it
us them

1 Check the correct sentence.
2 ______ the object pronouns.
3 ______ the subject pronouns.
4 ______ the subject and object pronouns.
5 ______ the incorrect sentence.
6 ______ the list.

# Review A

## GRAMMAR

Grammar Extra pages 104 and 106.

**1 Complete the table.**

| Subject | Verb (*be*) | Contraction | Negative | Question |
|---|---|---|---|---|
| I | am | I'm | I'm not | Am I ...? |
| You | | | | |
| He/She/It | | | | |
| We | | | | |
| They | | | | |

**2 Complete the conversation with *this* or *these*.**

**Officer:** Open your bag, please, sir.
**Man:** Yes, sure.
**Officer:** What's (1) this?
**Man:** It's an iPad.
**Officer:** Mm. And what are (2) _________?
**Man:** They're tickets.
**Officer:** Tickets? And what's (3)_________?
**Man:** It's a cell phone.
**Officer:** Ah, yes. What's (4) _________?
**Man:** It's a camera.
**Officer:** Oh, ... and what are (5) _________?
**Man:** They're tissues. I have a cold.
**Officer:** Fine. Thank you, sir.

1.49 **Listen and check.**

**3 Underline the correct answers.**

a There **is / are** a pool.
b **Are / Is** there any people?
c There **is / are** some rooms.
d **Are / Is** there a beach?

**4 Complete the table.**

| **Subject pronoun** | I | (2) _____ | he | (4) _____ | it | (6) _____ | they |
|---|---|---|---|---|---|---|---|
| **Possessive determiner** | (1) my | your | (3) _____ | her | (5) _____ | our | (7) _____ |

**5 Complete the sentences with the verbs in the present progressive form.**

a I (wear) 'm wearing a T-shirt.
b My parents (work) _______ today.
c I (sit) _________ near the door.
d I (read) _________ a newspaper.

**Rewrite the sentences in the negative.**

a I'm not wearing a T-shirt.

**Check (✓) the sentences which are true for you. Compare with a partner.**

**6 Write questions.**

a you / work? Do you work?
b your mother / like shopping?
c you and your family / eat together every day?
d you / have a Japanese car?

**7 Find the mistake! Cross out the incorrect sentence.**

1 a Is she Italian?
  b ~~She is Italian?~~

2 a What's this?
  b What's these?

3 a Is you're family from Mexico?
  b Is your family from Mexico?

4 a They likes Japanese food.
  b They like Japanese food.

## VOCABULARY

**1 Write the language of each country.**

a  Mexico
b  Brazil
c  Spain
d  Germany
e  China
f  Italy
g  Japan
h  the USA

**2 Write the telephone numbers as you say them.**

a 01779 4062 533 *oh one seven seven nine, four oh six two, five three three*
b 540-294-0056
c 020 1663 4156
d 410-239-8104

**3 Complete the questions with the words in the box.**

animal ~~actor~~ sport movie singer color

a Who's your favorite *actor*? Leonardo DiCaprio
b What's your favorite _________? *La La Land*
c Who's your favorite _________? Katy Perry
d What's your favorite _________? blue
e What's your favorite _________? basketball
f What's your favorite _________? tiger

**Take turns asking and answering the questions with a partner.**

**4 Complete the descriptions with the words in the box.**

~~T-shirt~~ tie belt shirt jeans rings sneakers shoes suit

She's wearing a white (1) *T-shirt* and a pair of (2) _________ with a brown (3) _________. She's wearing a pair of white (4) _________ and she has a lot of (5) _________ on her fingers.
He's wearing a dark (6) _________, a white (7) _________, a red (8) _________, and a pair of beautiful Italian (9) _________.

**5 Write vowels (*a*, *e*, *i*, *o*, *u*) to complete the names of jobs.**

a d*o*ct*o*r
b h_ _rdr_ss_r
c p_l_c_ _ff_c_r
d d_nt_st
e s_l_s cl_rk
f t_x_ dr_v_r

## PRONUNCIATION

**1 Look at some words from Units 1-3. Say the words and add them to the table.**

~~Brazil~~ Chinese ~~hairdresser~~ dentist ~~doctor~~ Japan Portugal camera Italy officer

| A: ■ ▪ | B: ■ ▪ ▪ | C: ▪ ■ |
| --- | --- | --- |
| *doctor* | *hairdresser* | *Brazil* |

**2 Underline the stressed syllable in each word.**

1.50 **Listen, check, and repeat.**

## READING & LISTENING

**1 Read the text and answer the questions.**

a Who is the job profile of?
b What's her nationality?
c What's her job?
d What does she like?

aboutjobs.com/patriciakidman

**AboutJobs.com** Home About Jobs Profiles Contact us search

### Full Profile

**Name: Patricia Kidman**

My name's Patricia and I'm from the USA. I'm 28 and I live and work here in New York City.
I'm a teacher at the Kingston International School in Queens. I have three years teaching experience. I work six days a week, so it's hard work. I really like teaching, and I like meeting my new students every year and watching them grow and learn. My favorite subject is English – some of my students come from Mexico and Brazil so they need to learn the language.
I speak three languages – English, Spanish and Chinese. I like going out to eat, listening to hip-hop music, and traveling to new places.
I work hard but I also like relaxing. I'm looking for new teaching jobs. Please contact me here.

CONTACT

**2 Read the text again. Are the sentences true (T) or false (F)?**

a Patricia lives in New York City. [T]
b She works three days a week. [ ]
c Some of her students come from Brazil. [ ]
d She likes eating out. [ ]
e She doesn't like traveling to new places. [ ]
f She's looking for a relaxing job. [ ]

**3** 1.51 **Listen to a conversation between co-workers, Shelly and Jeff. They are discussing who to hire. Which person do they choose?**

**4 Listen again and complete the information about the three people.**

a
**AboutJobs.com**
**Mini Profile**

**Name:** ___________
**Age:** 24
**Nationality:** American
**Current job:** teacher
**Experience:** 1 year
**Likes:** sleeping, watching TV
**Phone:** 212-459-3125

b
**AboutJobs.com**
**Mini Profile**

**Name:** Marnie Williams
**Age:** 28
**Nationality:** British
**Current job:** ___________
**Experience:** 5 years
**Likes:** ___________, running
**Phone:** 44-21-456456

c
**AboutJobs.com**
**Mini Profile**

**Name:** Juan Cruz
**Age:** 29
**Nationality:** ___________
**Current job:** teacher
**Experience:** 6 years
**Likes:** swimming, watching movies, traveling
**Phone:** ___________

## WRITING & SPEAKING

1 **Match the punctuation features (a-e) with their names in the box.**

an apostrophe ☐ a capital letter ☐ a comma ☐ a period ☐ a question mark ☐

a .

b ,

c ?

d '

e A

2 **Complete the sentences with the names in Exercise 1.**

a You use ___a question mark___ at the end of a question.
b You use ____________ at the end of a sentence.
c You use ____________ to start a sentence and when you write names.
d You use ____________ to separate items in a list.
e You use ____________ for contractions or for possessions.

3 **Write questions in the correct order. Remember to start your questions with a capital letter and to use a question mark.**

a your / name / what's ?
What's your name?
b you / where / from / are ?
c old / how / you / are ?
d Brazil / from / you / are ?
e today / you / are / working ?
f like / English / do / you ?
g job / what / is / your ?

4 **Ask your partner the questions in Exercise 3.**

Where are you from?

I'm from the USA.

5 **Write about your partner, using the information you heard in Exercise 4. Then exchange texts with your partner. Check your partner's punctuation.**

This is my friend, William.
He's from the USA.

# 4 Living

## READING

1 **Look at the pictures and read the sentences. Guess which person the sentences describe. Underline *He* or *She*.**

a **He / She** lives in the city.
b **He / She** gets up early in the morning
c **He / She** does yoga in the morning.
d **He / She** has two or three cups of coffee in the morning.
e **He / She** goes to work by bike.
f **He / She** loves sports.
g **He / She** has a sleep in the afternoon.
h **He / She** falls asleep before it's dark.

**Hi, Sarah. It's Short Talk. Thanks for doing this.**
No problem, Short Talk.

**Where are you?**
I'm at my apartment. I'm making my breakfast at the moment.

**So, Sarah, tell us about yourself.**
I'm a model and I live here in Rio. I'm a real city girl. I always get up early in the morning and do yoga. I have breakfast, but no coffee. I usually go to work by bike, but I sometimes take a taxi.

**What do you do when you aren't working?**
I love the beach, but I hardly ever have the time to go there. I love sports, especially tennis. And I like horseback riding – I go every weekend.

**Any bad habits ...?**
Mm, let me see. I don't always eat a proper lunch – I'm too busy! I don't smoke and I don't usually drink too much alcohol. But I can be lazy. On Sundays, after I do the shopping, I hardly ever get off my couch.

**Thanks, Sarah, for your time this morning.**
Bye, Short Talk!

**Hi, Paul. It's Short Talk. How are you today?**
I'm good, Short Talk.

**So, where are you?**
I live in a research station in the Amazon. In the Madre de Dios area. I'm alone here right now. I love being alone in the wild.

**Wow! On your own? Isn't that lonely?**
No, I never get lonely. There are a lot of animals and insects here. They make a lot of noise.

**So, tell us about your day.**
Well, I usually get up very early. I usually watch the sun rise. I always have two or three cups of coffee. I work until lunch, and I sometimes have a short sleep in the afternoon. At night, I usually read or just listen to the sounds of the jungle.

**Do you sleep well there?**
Oh, yes, I often fall asleep before it's dark!

**Thanks for your time, Paul.**
You're welcome, Short Talk.

1.52 **Listen and check your answers.**

2 **Work with a partner. Make questions from the sentences in Exercise 1.**

Bobby, do you get up early in the morning?
No, I don't.

**Write your own Q & A.**

*Do you get up early in the morning?*
*No, I don't. I sleep late.*

- **Grammar:** Simple present. Adverbs of frequency. Time. Prepositions of time.
- **Vocabulary:** Verb phrases: *make* and *do*. Ordinal numbers. Months. Dates. Seasons.
- **Language for Life:** Enquiring

## VOCABULARY

**1 Complete the verb phrases with *make* or *do*.**

| a ________ | b ________ |
|---|---|
| (my) homework | a lot of noise |
| the housework | breakfast |
| the shopping | long telephone calls |
| the laundry | the beds |
| the dishes | the decisions |

1.53 **Listen, check, and repeat.**

**2 At home, who does or makes the things in Exercise 1? Make sentences and compare with your partner.**

My sister does her homework.
My brother makes a lot of noise.

## GRAMMAR

**1 Complete the chart with the adverbs of frequency highlighted in the article on page 30.**

a ________ b ________ c often d ________ e hardly ever f ________

100% ............................................ 0%

1.54 **Listen and check.**

**Adverbs of frequency**

**Adverbs go before main verbs:**

She **hardly ever** goes out.
He doesn't **usually** drink.
Do you **ever** walk to work?

**Adverbs go after *be*:**

I'm **always** at home.
He's **never** late.

**2 Add an adverb of frequency to make the sentences true for you.**

a I wake up before the sun rises. I hardly ever wake up before the sun rises.
b I take a short sleep in the afternoon.
c I visit my relatives on weekends.
d I'm at home in the evening.
e I drink alcohol when I go out.

**3 Find out your partner's answers. Ask questions with *Do you ever ...?* or *Are you ever ...?***

Do you ever wake up before the sun rises?

No, hardly ever.

**4 Pairwork Student A:** page 97 **Student B:** page 101

**5 Grammar Extra 4** page 106. Read the explanation and do the exercises.

## PRONUNCIATION

**1** 1.55 **Listen and repeat the ordinal numbers.**

**2** 1.56 **Check (✓) the group of ordinal numbers you hear.**

| | | | | |
|---|---|---|---|---|
| a | $1^{st}$ $2^{nd}$ $3^{rd}$ | ✓ | $3^{rd}$ $2^{nd}$ $1^{st}$ | ☐ |
| b | $2^{nd}$ $6^{th}$ $7^{th}$ | ☐ | $7^{th}$ $6^{th}$ $2^{nd}$ | ☐ |
| c | $4^{th}$ $5^{th}$ $1^{st}$ | ☐ | $5^{th}$ $1^{st}$ $4^{th}$ | ☐ |
| d | $10^{th}$ $12^{th}$ $20^{th}$ | ☐ | $10^{th}$ $20^{th}$ $12^{th}$ | ☐ |

**Ordinal numbers**

1st = first
2nd = second
3rd = third
4th = fourth
5th = fifth
6th = sixth
7th = seventh
8th = eighth
9th = ninth
10th = tenth

## LANGUAGE FOR LIFE

1 1.64 **Read and listen to the conversations (a-c) and match them with the pictures (1-3).**

**a**

**Customer:** Hello!
**Clerk:** Sorry, we're closed.
**Customer:** What time do you open?
**Clerk:** We open at nine o'clock.
**Customer:** But it's nine o'clock now.
**Clerk:** No, it isn't. It's 8:58.

**b**

**Bob:** Oh, Jenny, we don't have any milk, and the grocery store is closed
**Jenny:** The 7-11 is open.
**Bob:** Oh, what time does it open?
**Jenny:** Seven o'clock.
**Bob:** And what time does it close?
**Jenny:** Eleven o'clock.
**Bob:** Ah, yes. Seven-eleven!

**c**

**Clerk:** Good morning, Bling Jewelry.
**Customer:** Oh, hello. What time do you close?
**Clerk:** We close at 5:30, ma'am.
**Customer:** And what about on Sunday?
**Clerk:** I'm sorry, we're closed on Sunday.
**Customer:** Oh, no – I work until six every day except Sunday.

1

2

3

2 **Write the useful phrases correctly with the words in parenthesis.**

a What time you open? (do)
*What time do you open?*
b We open nine o'clock. (at)
c What time it open? (does)
d What time it close? (does)
e What time you close? (do)
f We close 5:30. (at)
g We're closed Sunday. (on)

1.65 **Listen, check, and repeat the expressions.**

3 **Work with a partner. Practice the conversation.**

4 **Work with a partner. Ask about opening and closing times in your city. Use the ideas in the box.**

the grocery store a restaurant
the school your bank a bar

### Life Skills: People Management

Working with Others

1 **Read these sentences about co-workers. Order (1-6). 1 – really bad; 6 – not so bad.**

a

b

c

d

e

f

a He's always late for meetings. ☐
b He sometimes takes his shoes off in the office. ☐
c He never opens the door for female co-workers. ☐
d She usually puts on her make up at her desk. ☐
e She sometimes says bad things about her co-workers. ☐
f He always speaks very loudly in the office. ☐

2 **Compare your answers with a partner.**

3 **Choose a phrase you would use to talk to your co-workers. Practice with your partner.**

Please can you be here on time?
Do you mind putting your shoes on?

*Could you stop …?*
*Do you mind (not) …?*
*Please can you …?*
*Can I ask you to …?*

MACMILLAN LIFE SKILLS

# 4 Vocabulary Extra

## Times of the year & dates

**1 Match the pictures with the seasons.**

fall __3__ spring ______ summer ______ winter ______

**2 Write the words or numbers.**

| 1st = first | 9th = | = seventeenth | 25th = |
|---|---|---|---|
| 2nd = | 10th = | 18th = | = twenty-sixth |
| 3rd = | 11th = | 19th = | 27th = |
| 4th = | = twelfth | = twentieth | 28th = |
| = fifth | 13th = | 21st = | 29th = |
| 6th = | 14th = | = twenty-second | = thirtieth |
| 7th = | 15th = | 23rd = | 31st = |
| = eighth | = sixteenth | 24th = | |

**3 Complete the months of the year.**

1 Janu*ary* 2 Feb______ 3 Mar______ 4 Apr______ 5 May 6 Ju______

7 Ju______ 8 Aug______ 9 Sept______ 10 Oct______ 11 Nov______ 12 Dec______

**4 Complete the days of the week.**

S*unday*____ M__________ Tu__________ W__________ Th__________ F__________ Sa__________

## Focus on *go*

go for a walk go running go on the internet go shopping ~~go to bed~~ go to work

**1 Complete the table with phrases in the box.**

| Some uses of go | Examples | | | |
|---|---|---|---|---|
| **a** *go to* + place | go to Spain | go to school | (1) *go to bed* | (2) ________ |
| **b** *go* + *ing* = do an activity | go swimming | go dancing | (3) ________ | (4) ________ |
| **c** *go* + *for a* + noun = do an activity | go for a drink | go for dinner | (5) ________ | |
| **d** verb phrases with *go* | go out every Saturday night | go on a vacation | (6) ________ | |

**2 Write your own example sentences for each use of *go.***

# 5 Ocean

## VOCABULARY & LISTENING

**1** 1.66 **Listen and repeat the names of the different water sports.**

a windsurfing

b scuba diving

c kitesurfing

d fishing

e surfing

f sailing

g swimming

**2** 1.67 **Listen to two interviews about water sports. Circle the time expressions you hear in each interview.**

| | Pam | Steven |
|---|---|---|
| went swimming | a in 2006 / in August | c on Monday / yesterday |
| went sailing | | d a long time ago / three days ago |
| went windsurfing | b last week / last summer | |
| went scuba diving | | e last year / last month |

**3 Complete the table on how to use *ago*.**

| ***on, in,* and *last*** | | ***ago*** |
|---|---|---|
| a last week | = | *a week* ago |
| b on Saturday | = | ________ days ago |
| c last August | = | ________ month(s) ago |
| d in 2002 | = | ________ years ago |
| e in ________ | = | ten years ago |
| f on ________ | = | three days ago |

**4 Which water sports do you like? Ask your partner.**

- **Grammar:** Simple past: regular/irregular affirmative forms
- **Vocabulary:** Water sports. Time expressions/linkers.
- **Language for Life:** The weather

## GRAMMAR

**1 Rewrite two questions from the interview on page 36.**

a ever / you / go / Do / swimming?
b the last time / was / When / went / you / swimming?

1.68 **Listen, check, and repeat.**

**2 Ask your partner more questions about past activities. Use words and phrases in the box or your own ideas.**

dancing shopping skiing to the beach to the theater windsurfing

Do you ever go windsurfing?

Yes, I do.

When was the last time you went windsurfing?

Last summer.

**Simple past**

| | be | go |
|---|---|---|
| I | was | went |
| You | were | went |
| He | was | went |
| She | was | went |
| It | was | went |
| We | were | went |
| They | were | went |

## READING

**1** 1.69 **Read the article. Which do you think is the best title?**

a The Birth of a Company
b We Met In 1969

**2 Are these sentences true or false?**

a Brian and Claw were friends before they started a company. True
b Brian was a science teacher when he met Claw.
c They rented an old shoe shop for $10 a week.
d Alan Green joined the company in December 1969.
e The company has 2,500 employees around the world.

ripcurl.com

My Account Wishlist My Cart

Home Products About Contact

RIPCURL

# About

In March of 1969, two surfing friends, Doug "Claw" Warbrick and Brian Singer, met in Torquay, Australia. Claw didn't have a job and Brian was a science teacher.

They talked about surfing, and then Claw asked the question that changed their lives … "Do you want to start making surfboards?" he asked.

Brian said, "Yes!" and stopped teaching a couple of days later and Claw and Brian started the surf company, Rip Curl.

Brian worked in a garage, so in April 1969, they made their first surfboards there. In these early days, Claw and Brian made four surfboards a week.

By November, they needed a bigger place. They rented the Old Torquay Bakery for $10 a week. They increased production to 12 surfboards a week.

In December, another local surfer, Alan Green, joined, and they started making Rip Curl wetsuits too.

This was just the start. Rip Curl now has 2,500 employees in Australia and is a global surfing brand.

## GRAMMAR

1 **Label the boxes *Regular verbs* or *Irregular verbs*.**

| a ____________ | b ____________ |
|---|---|
| call - called | can - could |
| like - liked | drive - drove |
| play - played | fall - fell |
| stop - stopped | make - made |
| study - studied | put - put |
| watch - watched | sit - sat |

**Simple past**

| | Regular (work) | Irregular (have) |
|---|---|---|
| I | work**ed** | had |
| You | work**ed** | had |
| He | work**ed** | had |
| She | work**ed** | had |
| It | work**ed** | had |
| We | work**ed** | had |

2 **Match the phrases to make rules about forming regular past forms.**

| | |
|---|---|
| **a** Most regular verbs *(watch)* | add *d (liked)* |
| **b** Verbs ending in *e (like)* | add a consonant + *ed (stopped)* |
| **c** Verbs ending in consonant + *y (study)* | add *ed (watched)* |
| **d** Verbs ending in vowel + consonant *(stop)* | delete *y* and add *ied (studied)* |

3 **Write the past tenses for these regular verbs.**

**a** ask ___asked___
**b** chat ________
**c** finish ________
**d** smile ________
**e** start ________

1.70 **Listen, check, and repeat.**

4 **Complete the verbs with the irregular past forms in the box.**

| | | | | | |
|---|---|---|---|---|---|
| **a** go | ___went___ | do | ___did___ | send | ___sent___ |
| **b** hold | ________ | sell | ________ | tell | ________ |
| **c** think | ________ | catch | ________ | hear | ________ |
| **d** take | ________ | break | ________ | speak | ________ |
| **e** tear | ________ | come | ________ | wear | ________ |
| **f** read | ________ | say | ________ | give | ________ |

broke came caught ~~did~~
gave heard held read said
~~sent~~ sold spoke thought
told took tore ~~went~~ wore

1.71 **Listen, check, and repeat.**

5 **Practice saying the past forms of the verbs in Exercise 4. Circle the past form with the different sound in each group.**

**a** went (did) sent

1.72 **Listen, check, and repeat.**

6 **Pairwork Student A:** page 97 **Student B:** page 101

7 **Grammar Extra 5** page 106. Read the explanation and do the exercises.

## PRONUNCIATION

1 **Say the present and past forms of the verbs in the box. Which verbs have an extra syllable in the past form? Complete the table.**

~~ask - asked~~ love - loved ~~point - pointed~~
start - started stop - stopped use - used
want - wanted work - worked

| A: No extra syllables | B: Extra syllable |
|---|---|
| ■ → ■ | ■ → ■ ▪ |
| ask – asked | point – pointed |
| | |
| | |
| | |

1.73 **Listen, check, and repeat.**

## READING & VOCABULARY

1 1.74 **Read the story. Are the following sentences true or false?**

a David Samuels is from Portugal. *False*

b David Samuels went surfing last month. ________

c Samuels fell because of a shark. ________

d Bob Bennett tried to help. ________

e A third man fell into the water. ________

f They were safe on a jet ski. ________

YouTube search

### Big Waves, Lucky Escape

Epic Waves

Subscribe 10 K

12 304 views

Add to Share More 564 32

This new video on social media shows American surfer David Samuels' accident when he was surfing giant waves in Portugal.

One day last month, Samuels was surfing some very big waves. After an hour, the waves got even bigger. The video starts at this point. Suddenly, Samuels fell and went underwater. No one could see him. A surfer friend on the beach, Bob Bennett, had a jet ski and he rode into the ocean to help. At first, Bennett couldn't find Samuels. The waves were very big and dangerous. Eventually, Bennet found Samuels and Samuels got on the jet ski — but another wave hit them. The jet ski fell over and both men went into the water. Ten minutes later, the two surfers swam out of the waves. As you can see on the video, they were very tired, but happy to be alive!

Two weeks later, Samuels and Bennett surfed in the same place. It was dangerous, but the waves were great!

2 **Use the highlighted time linkers from the story to complete the story below.**

1.75 **Listen and check.**

A man and woman went on vacation to the Indian Ocean. (1) *One day*, they went on a boat with twenty other people and went scuba diving. The boat stopped in the middle of the ocean, and everyone went diving. (2) ________, everyone returned to the boat, and the boat went back to the port.

But the man and woman didn't return to the boat. When they finished diving, there was no boat. (3) ________, they shouted, but no one heard them. They waited and waited for the boat to return, but (4) ________ they realized they were alone.

(5) ________, something moved near them under the water. (6) ________, a fisherman found their camera.

3 **In your opinion, what happened to the man and the woman?**

## LANGUAGE FOR LIFE

1 1.76 **Read and listen to the conversations (a-c). Match the conversations with a sport in the box.**

fishing running sailing skiing swimming windsurfing

**a**
**Alan:** Hello.
**Mom:** Hi, how are you?
**Alan:** Good.
**Mom:** How's the weather?
**Alan:** It's sunny and very windy.
**Mom:** Oh, that's a shame.
**Alan:** No, it's great. I want to go windsurfing. How's the weather at home?
**Mom:** It's cloudy, it's raining, and it's cold.
**Alan:** Oh, sorry.

**b**
**Kelly:** Dad?
**Dad:** Hi, honey. How are you doing?
**Kelly:** Not very good.
**Dad:** Why?
**Kelly:** It's sunny and warm. There isn't any snow.
**Dad:** Ah.
**Kelly:** How's the weather at home?
**Dad:** It's snowing.
**Kelly:** Oh, no!

**c**
**Eric:** Hello.
**Janice:** Hello. Did you catch any fish?
**Eric:** No.
**Janice:** Where are you?
**Eric:** I'm not sure ... It's very foggy.

2 **Complete the table with words from the conversations in Exercise 1.**

| Nouns | Expressions |
|---|---|
| | How's the (1) weather? |
| sun | It's (2) ________. |
| wind | It's (3) ________. |
| cloud | It's (4) ________. |
| rain | It's (5) ________. |
| snow | It's (6) ________. |
| fog | It's (7) ________. |

1.77 **Listen, check, and repeat.**

3 **Work with a partner. Practice the conversations in Exercise 1.**

### Life Skills: Problem-solving

A Vacation Nightmare

1 **Complete the sentences using the words in the box.**

~~last month~~ nine o'clock twenty-three last week four three days

a The hotel ran out of money last month.
b The hotel has ________ rooms.
c The beach was closed ________.
d The last flight left at ________ this morning.
e There are no flights for ________.
f There are only ________ taxis on the island.

1.78 **Listen and check.**

2 **Work with a partner. Look at the options. Create a pro (+) and con (-) list for one of the options. Decide on the best option.**

**Option A** Try and find a new hotel.
**Option B** Wait at the airport and fly home in three days.
**Option C** Go to the hotel and share a room with other travelers.
**Option D** Find a beach and camp there.

OPTION A

| Pro (+) | Con (-) |
|---|---|
| More rooms | More money |

3 **Listen to other pairs in the class and make a list of all the options.**

# 5 Vocabulary Extra

## Sports

1 **Match the pictures with the sports.**

| | | | |
|---|---|---|---|
| ______ cycling | ______ kitesurfing | ______ scuba diving | ______ swimming |
| ______ fishing | ______ running | ______ soccer | ______ tennis |
| ______ horseback riding | ______ sailing | ______ surfing | ______ windsurfing |

2 **Work with a partner. Cover the words. Look at the pictures. Ask and answer questions.**

What sport is number 1?

Surfing.

## Focus on *make* and *do*

1 **Complete the table with the words in the box.**

a decision   a noise   ~~dinner~~   exercise
my homework   the dishes

| ***make* and *do*** | **Examples** | | | | |
|---|---|---|---|---|---|
| **a** make ... | coffee | a mistake | (1) dinner | (2) | (3) |
| **b** do ... | the shopping | the housework | (4) | (5) | (6) |

2 **Write six of your own example sentences for these expressions with *make* and *do*.**

# 6 Alone

## VOCABULARY

1 **Listen and repeat the adjectives in the box. Check (✓) the words you know.**

angry   bored   embarrassed   excited   scared   happy   nervous   sad   worried

1.79 **Listen, check, and repeat.**

2 **Work with a partner. Find one or more adjectives in the box in Exercise 1 to describe the person's feelings in each picture.**

## SPEAKING

1 **How do you feel in the different situations described in the box?**

in a fast car   in a nightclub   in a plane   now
when you see a baby   when you see a spider   when you sing karaoke
when you speak English   when you take an exam

**Ask your partner.**

How do you feel when you take an exam?

Really nervous.

Me, too.

- **Grammar:** Simple past: affirmative, negative, and question forms
- **Vocabulary:** Feelings. Adjectives. *Wh*-questions.
- **Language for Life:** Complaints and suggestions

## READING & WRITING

**1** 1.80 **Read the blog about Katie Spotz and answer the questions.**

a Where did she start? b Where did she go?

blogger.com

Blogger View Blog

Post Katie Spotz Publish Save Preview Close

Post Settings: Labels, Schedule, Permalink, Location, Options

**Day 1**
Katie started her journey in Dakar, Senegal. She became the first person to row the Atlantic Ocean alone at the age of 22. Her boat, 'Live', was a 19-foot yellow wooden rowboat.

**Day 26**
It was hard for Katie to sleep because of the 20-foot waves. She wasn't scared of the big waves because her boat was okay even in 50-foot waves.

**Day 30**
After a month, Katie realized she was only halfway across the ocean. She wasn't happy about it, but after that, she made good progress. She traveled 60 kilometers a day.

**Day 62**
Katie decided to row for an extra 8 days. The wind was very strong and it was impossible to stop in Cayenne, French Guiana. So she rowed to Georgetown, Guyana. Katie traveled 640 kilometers more, and she was very tired.

**Day 69**
Almost a disaster! Katie smelled smoke. Her GPS tracker was on fire. Luckily, she was able to put it out.

**Day 70**
After 70 days, 5 hours, and 22 minutes on the Atlantic Ocean, Spotz arrived in Georgetown, Guyana, in South America. She did it! And she collected $70,000 for charity — what a hero!

**2 Match the words to complete the information.**

| A | B |
|---|---|
| a Katie | rowboat |
| b $70,000 | hours |
| c 70 | days |
| d 19-foot | waves |
| e 5 | 22 years-old |
| f 20-foot | charity |

**3 Use the information from Exercise 2 to make sentences about the text.**

a *Katie was twenty-two years old.*

**4 Write three blog entries of a long journey you have experienced.**

*Day One: We left from New York. It was snowing.*

**Read your entries to your partner.**

## LISTENING & VOCABULARY

**1** 1.81 **Listen to a podcast about Katie Spotz. Underline the correct information.**

a Katie **was / wasn't** nervous about the big waves.
b Katie's family **was / wasn't** worried about her.
c Katie **was / wasn't** happy about finishing in Georgetown.
d Katie **was / wasn't** scared of running out of food.

**2 Complete the sentences with the prepositions in the box.**

~~about~~ about in of with

a I'm worried *about* my future.
b I'm never angry ________ my friends.
c I'm scared ________ snakes.
d I'm not interested ________ modern art.
e I'm not embarrassed ________ my English.

1.82 **Listen, check, and repeat.**

**3 Check the sentences that are true for you. Compare with your partner.**

## READING

1 1.83 **Read about Syd Barrett. What band did he start with a friend?**

celebrities.com

# celebrities.com

Home Latest stories Photos search

previous
Emily Dickinson

## Top Ten Reclusive Celebrities!
Number Five
### Shine On: Syd Barrett

next
Greta Garbo

The rock band Pink Floyd is a very successful band, they have sold over 250 million albums. But one of the original members didn't stay in the band very long and he never became rich and successful.

Syd Barrett was born in Cambridge, UK, and met musician Roger Waters at school there. They formed Pink Floyd in 1965. For the next two years, Pink Floyd played many concerts and released two albums. But Syd quit in 1968, and between then and 1970 he recorded two solo albums.

Syd got sick and moved to London where he lived in a hotel. People rarely saw him. In 1978, he walked nearly 50 miles to his mother's house in Cambridge because he did not have any money. Syd began to use his birth name of Roger and spent the rest of his life painting, gardening, and writing a book on art history that was never published.

Over the years, there were only a couple of photos of Syd. He died, alone, at 60.

2 **Put the lines in the correct order.**

a Syd met Roger Waters at school. ☐
b Syd recorded two solo albums. ☐
c Syd Barrett left Pink Floyd. ☐
d Syd started using the name 'Roger'. ☐
e Syd Barrett was born in Cambridge. 1
f Syd died aged 60. ☐
g Pink Floyd was formed in 1965. ☐
h Syd walked from London to Cambridge. ☐

1.84 **Listen and check.**

## WRITING

1 **Think about a retired person you know well.**
**Write an article (similar to a Wikipedia entry) about their life using the verb phrases in the box.**

- was born in ... (a place, a year)
- went to ... (school, college)
- left ... (school, college)
- worked as a/an ... (job)
- moved to ... (a new place)
- lived in ... (a place)
- met ... (a person)
- got married to ... (a person)
- got divorced from ... (a person)
- had ... children
- retired

2 **Compare your article with a partner.**

## GRAMMAR

1 **Complete the questions and answers about you and your family.**

a Did you go to elementary school near here? Yes, I did. No, I didn't.
b Did you walk to school? Yes, I did. No, I didn't.
c ____ you move when you were a child? ________ ________
d ____ your father leave school at sixteen? ________ ________
e ____ your mother study English at school? ________ ________
f ____ your parents go to college? ________ ________

1.85 **Listen, check, and repeat.**

2 **Work with your partner. Ask and answer the questions in Exercise 1.**

3 **Pairwork Student A:** page 97 **Student B:** page 101

4 **Grammar Extra 6** page 108. Read the explanation and do the exercises.

### Simple past

I
You
He
She
It
We
They

**worked.**
**didn't work.**

**went.**
**didn't go.**

**Did** you work/go?
Yes, I **did**.
No, I **didn't**.

## PRONUNCIATION

1 **Complete lists A and B with the simple past form of the irregular verbs.**

| A | | B | |
|---|---|---|---|
| know | knew | break | |
| mean | | fly | flew |
| tear | | spend | |
| speak | | teach | |
| think | | wear | |

1.86 **Listen, check, and repeat.**

2 **Match a verb from list A with a verb from list B with a similar sound.**

knew → flew

1.87 **Listen, check, and repeat.**

### Question forms

**Where ...?** = place
**Who ...?** = people
**When ...?** = time
**What ...?** = object or activity
**How ...?** = in what way

## SPEAKING: ANECDOTE

1 1.88 **Listen to Laura talking about her last summer vacation. Underline the correct information.**

a Where did you go? I went **to the beach / to the mountains.**
b When did you go there? I went **last month / in July.**
c Who did you go with? I went **with my family / alone.**
d How did you get there? I went **by train / by plane and by car.**
e Where did you stay? I stayed **in a hotel / with friends.**
f How long did you stay? I stayed **for two weeks / a month.**
g What did you do all day? I **visited a small town / went to the beach.**
h What did you do in the evening? I went **out to the bars and clubs / shopping.**

2 **You are going to tell your partner about your last vacation.**

- Ask yourself the questions in Exercise 1.
- Think about *what* to say and *how* to say it.
- Tell your partner about your last vacation.

Last summer I went to ...

## LANGUAGE FOR LIFE

1 1.89 **Read and listen to the conversations (a-d) and match them with the pictures (1-4).**

1 

2 

3 

4 

a **Nick:** I'm thirsty.
**Monica:** Me, too – let's have a cup of coffee.
**Nick:** Coffee? No, thanks. I'd like a beer!

b **Sam:** I'm bored.
**Mom:** Why don't you read a book?
**Sam:** A book? No, thanks!

c **Alicia:** I'm hungry. Is it lunchtime?
**Brigit:** No, it's eleven thirty. Why don't you eat some fruit?
**Alicia:** No, thanks. Do you have any chocolate?

d **Bob:** I'm tired.
**Sue:** Me, too. Let's stay at home tonight.
**Bob:** Good idea. There's baseball on TV.

2 1.90 **Listen and repeat the expressions.**

a I'm thirsty.
b Let's have a cup of coffee.
c I'm bored.
d Why don't you read a book?
e I'm hungry.
f I'm tired.
g Me, too.

3 **Complete these conversations with phrases from Exercise 2.**

a ___I'm bored.___
Why don't you go out with your friends?

b ______________
Why don't you have a snack?

c ______________
Me, too. Let's stream a movie tonight.

d ______________
Why don't you have an early lunch?

e ______________
Me, too. Let's have coffee.

f ______________
Why don't you play on your computer?

1.91 **Listen, check, and repeat.**

4 **Work with a partner. Write similar conversations to the ones in Exercise 1. Use the problems in the box or your own ideas.**

**Practice your conversation.**

I'm cold I'm hot. I'm scared of flying.
I'm worried about my exams.

### Life Skills: Self-knowledge
Emotions

1 **Are you an angry person? Take the test.**

**How do you feel?**
**fine: (0 pts)**
**slightly angry: (1 pt)**
**angry: (2 pts)**
**very angry: (3 pts)**

You failed an exam. ☐
You lost your wallet. ☐
You missed the train. ☐
You dropped your coffee. ☐
Your boss shouted at you. ☐
You got stuck in a traffic jam. ☐

**Are you an angry person?**
***No* = less than 10 pts, *Yes* = over 10 pts**

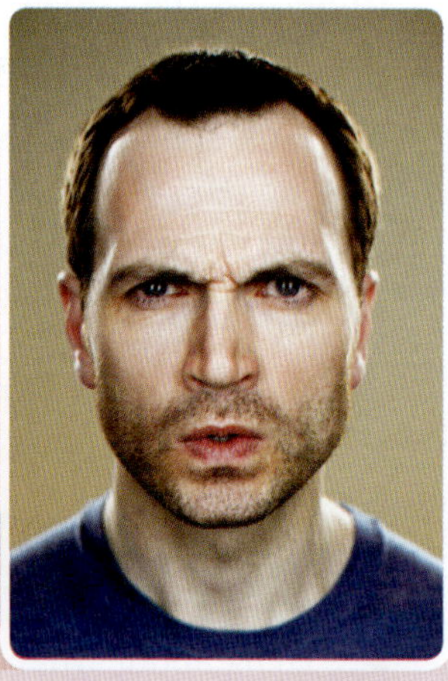

2 **What other things make you angry? Make a list and compare with a partner.**

3 **What can you say to an angry person? Choose an expression and practice with your partner.**

Calm down!

It's not so bad!

Chill out!

# 6 Vocabulary Extra

## Feelings

**1 Match the pictures with the feelings.**

| | | | |
|---|---|---|---|
| __4__ She's angry. | ______ He's embarrassed. | ______ She's very interested. | ______ He's scared. |
| ______ He's bored. | ______ They're excited. | ______ She's sad. | ______ She's worried. |

**2 Match the sentence beginnings in Exercise 1 with the sentence endings below.**

*4 – f She's angry with her son.*

**a** ... about his body.
**b** ... about her future.
**c** ... about their vacation.
**d** ... about going.
**e** ... in horses.
**f** ... with her son.
**g** ... of dogs.
**h** ... with her job.

## Focus on the weather

**1 Match the pictures with the words.**

| | | | |
|---|---|---|---|
| It's cloudy. __6__ | It's foggy. ______ | It's raining. ______ | It's sunny. ______ |
| It's cold. ______ | It's hot. ______ | It's snowing. ______ | It's windy. ______ |

**2 How's the weather?**

# Review B

## GRAMMAR

Grammar Extra pages 106 and 108.

**1 Complete the sentences with the simple present forms of the verbs in the box.**

do get up go have live ~~work~~

a I __work__ from 9:00 a.m. to 5:00 p.m.
b My mother ________ to the store on Fridays.
c We __________ near the station.
d Sue __________ exercise after work.
e John and Ella ________ early in the morning.
f Pete __________ breakfast at work.

**Write sentences in the negative.**

a *I don't work from 9:00 a.m. to 5:00 p.m.*

**2 Put the words in the correct order.**

a a nap / I / sometimes / at work / take
b make / long telephone calls / never / I
c my bed / I / make / always
d listen / hardly ever / I / to reggae
e I / go / often / to the gym
f usually / have / I / with my family / dinner

**Change the sentences to make them true for you.**

a *I never take a nap at work.*

**3 Complete the table with the phrases in the box. Which phrases in the box can come after *last*?**

~~the evening~~ 1997 Wednesday 8:15 night March 10 the summer July Thursday morning the morning eleven o'clock the weekend

| at | in | on |
|---|---|---|
| | *the evening* | |
| | | |
| | | |
| | | |

**4 Complete the story. Use the verbs in the box in the simple past form.**

~~ask~~ not be go have jump lose save see sit think

Pablo (1) __asked__ Kylie to go out with him last Saturday. They (2) __________ lunch on the beach. Pablo (3) __________ on Kylie's sunglasses! Kylie (4) __________ very happy. In the afternoon, Kylie (5) __________ swimming. Pablo (6) __________ something in the water. He (7) __________ it was a shark! But it was only a dolphin. Pablo (8) __________ into the water. He (9) __________ his glasses. A lifeguard (10) __________ him.

## VOCABULARY

**1 Write the months of the year.**

a The first month of the year. J<u>anuary</u>

b The seventh month of the year. J________

c The second month of the year. F________

d The month before September. A________

**2 Look at the pictures. Label the pictures with *make* or *do* and the words in the box.**

~~the dishes~~ a telephone call the housework homework

a do the dishes

b ________

c ________

d ________

**Work with a partner. Ask questions with *When was the last time you made/did ...?***

When was the last time you did the dishes?

**3 Write the dates in words.**

a 1/6 January sixth

b 2/22 ________

c 3/15 ________

d 11/8 ________

e 12/31 ________

f 4/5 ________

**4 Complete the words for water sports with *a, e, i, o, u*.**

a f<u>i</u>sh<u>i</u>ng

b k__t__ s__rf__ng

c s__ __l__ng

d sc__b__ d__v__ng

e s__rf__ng

f sw__mm__ng

g w__nds__rf__ng

## PRONUNCIATION

**1 Look at some words from Units 4-6. Say the words and add them to the table.**

~~August~~ ~~windsurfing~~ ~~embarrassed~~ excited always nervous November October surfing September terrible fishing usually worried

| A: ■▪ |
|---|
| <u>Au</u>gust |
| B: ■▪▪ |
| <u>wind</u>surfing |
| C: ▪■▪ |
| em<u>bar</u>rassed |

**2 <u>Underline</u> the stressed syllable in each word.**

1.92 **Listen, check, and repeat.**

## READING & LISTENING

1 **Work with a partner. Discuss the questions.**

a What do you do for charity?
b Do you know of any celebrities who help charities? Who are they and what do they support?

2 1.93 **Read the text and complete with the words in the box.**

Harry Potter | Star Trek | ~~One Direction~~ | Thor

celebrities.com

**celebrities.com** Home | Latest stories | Photos | search

◀ previous **Top 30 Generous Celebrities** next ▶

**No. 20 Louis Tomlinson & Niall Horan**
Two singers, Louis and Niall, played in a celebrity soccer game for Soccer Aid. The (1) <u>One Direction</u> boys joined other celebrities including the singer Robbie Williams and actor Damian Lewis at the game. People gave $6 million for UNICEF – just for this one soccer game! Great job, boys. Oh, and Louis' team won!

**No. 17 Chris Hemsworth**
The star of (2) ____________ and *Ghostbusters*, and who is, of course, (3) ____________ from the Marvel movies, is very worried about our oceans. Chris Hemsworth visited the Maldives to show people the problem – the plastic in our oceans. Chris helped clean beaches and collected bottles and other plastic trash. This superhero wants to make a difference to our oceans.

**No. 9 Emma Watson**
The British star from the (4) ____________ movies is always helping charities. Even when she was just a teenager, Watson worked with charities to stop global poverty. The actor helps women who are poorer than men. Many women in poor areas don't get an education because they have to look after their families. Emma is now a U.N. Women Goodwill Ambassador. Well done, Emma!

3 **Read the text again. Complete the sentences with information in the box.**

~~UNICEF~~ | Women | oceans | Maldives | Soccer | poverty

a Niall and Louis are raising money for <u>UNICEF</u>.
b Emma Watson is a U.N. ________ Goodwill Ambassador.
c Chris Hemsworth visited the ________ to support an ocean charity.
d Many famous people played in the ________ Aid game.
e Many women are in ________ because they don't get an education.
f Chris Hemsworth wants to help remove plastic from the ________.

4 1.94 **Listen to the news report about actor and writer David Walliams' charity swim. Complete the sentence.**

David swam from England to ________.

5 **Listen again. <u>Underline</u> the correct information.**

a Greg Whyte is David Walliams' **friend** / <u>**trainer**</u> / **brother**.
b David swam **14** / **24** / **34** kilometers.
c He arrived in France at **4:00 p.m.** / **5:00 p.m.** / **6:00 p.m.**
d After his swim, he felt very **happy** / **sad** / **angry**.

## WRITING & SPEAKING

**1 Read about a memorable day, and match the questions (a-f) with the answers (1-6).**

facebook.com

Tanya Home

Tanya Aliza
News Feed
Messenger

**EXPLORE**
Pages
Groups
Events
Friend List
Games
On This Day
Live Video
Pokes
Pages Feed
Suggested Edits
See More

**Tanya Aliza**
August 5 at 4:16 p.m.

**A memorable day**

My memorable day happened three years ago. I was in Rio de Janeiro. It was a beautiful, sunny day, and I went to Rock in Rio to see my favorite band. I only had one ticket, so I went alone. The concert was great, and the other fans were really nice. Later that evening, I went to a club, and the band was there! I spoke to them, and they gave me two free tickets for the next day. I was so happy!

Like Comment Share

24

Write a comment...

a When was it? ☐
b Where were you? ☐
c How was the weather? ☐
d Who were you with? ☐
e What did you do/see? ☐
f How did you feel at the end of the day? ☐

| | | |
|---|---|---|
| 1 Rio de Janeiro | 3 three years ago | 5 went alone |
| 2 spoke to my favorite band | 4 happy | 6 sunny |

**2 Work with a partner. Read the notes and complete the story of another memorable day.**

| | | |
|---|---|---|
| near Rome, Italy | ~~two years ago~~ | my boyfriend |
| won a dancing competition | tired | sunny |

My memorable day happened (1) two years ago. I was in a small town near (2) ______________, in (3) ______________. It was a hot, (4) ______________ day. I was with (5) ______________. We entered a (6) ______________ and we (7) ______________ first prize. At the end of the day, we were very (8) ______________, but it was a fantastic day.

**3 Think of a memorable day in your life. Answer the questions in note form.**

a When was it?
b Where were you?
c How was the weather?
d Who were you with?
e What did you do/see?
f How did you feel at the end of the day?

**4 From your notes, write a full story of a memorable day in your life.**

## READING & LISTENING

**1 Work with a partner. Look at the title and discuss the questions.**

**a** What is a diet?
**b** Do you think diets work? Why/Why not?

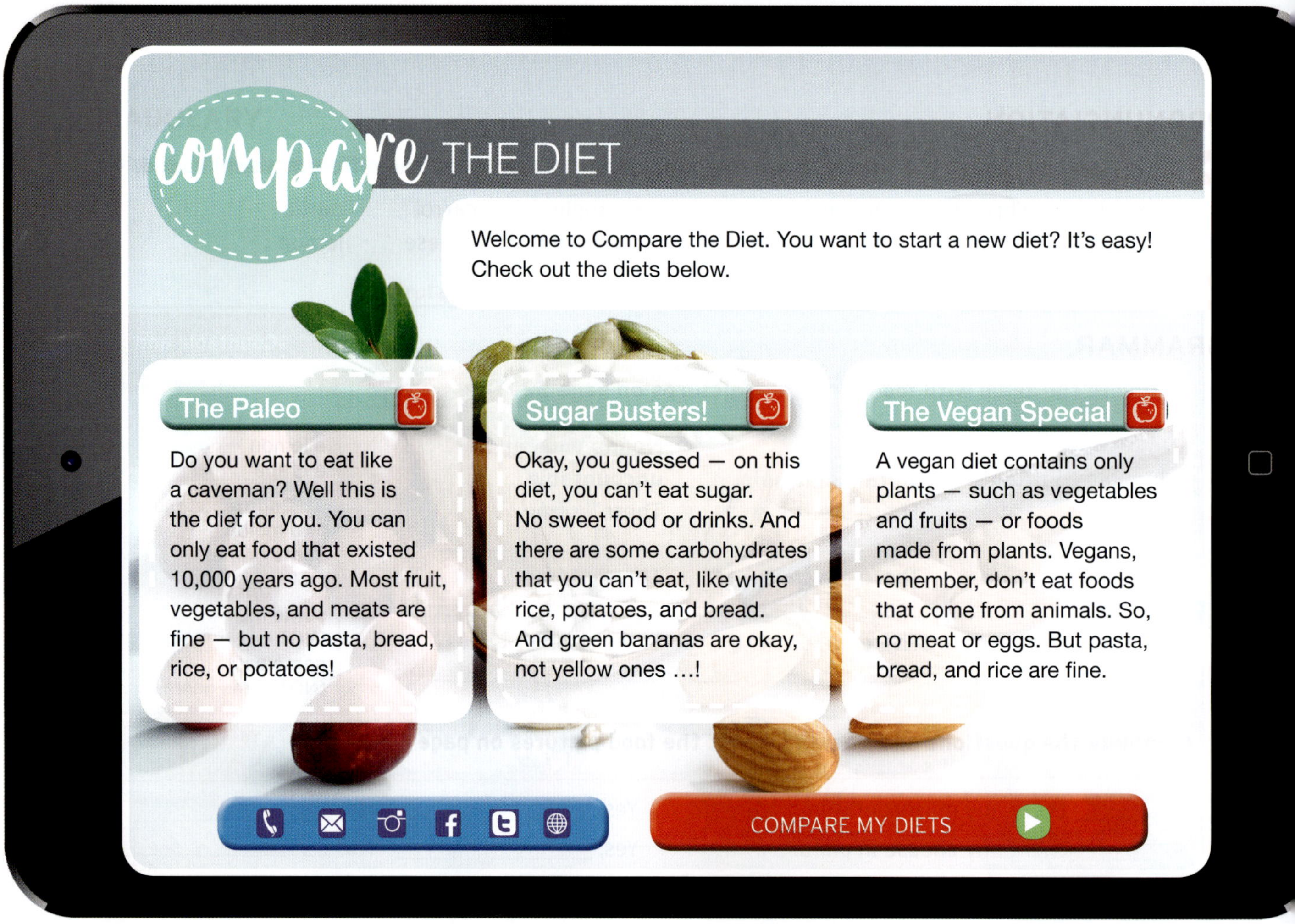


**2** 2.05 **Read and listen. Are these statements true or false?**

**a** You can eat meat on the Paleo diet. *True*
**b** You can eat pasta on the Vegan Special diet.
**c** You can eat yellow bananas on the Sugar Busters diet.
**d** You can eat potatoes on the Paleo and Vegan Special diets.
**e** You can't eat bread on any of these diets.

**3** 2.06 **Listen to a conversation between Ricardo and Gina. Confirm your answers to Exercise 2. What's Ricardo's new diet?**

## WRITING & SPEAKING

**Work with a partner. Use the diet information to complete the following tasks.**

**a** Write a menu for someone on the Vegan Special Diet.
**b** Write a menu for someone on the Paleo Diet.
**c** Decide which menu you like best.

# 7 Vocabulary Extra

## Food

**1 Match the pictures with the food in each group.**

**A** Fruit

______ an apple
______ a banana
______ grapes
______ a lemon
______ a mango
______ an orange
______ a pear
______ strawberries

**B** Vegetables

______ beans
______ a carrot
______ corn
______ garlic
______ mushrooms
______ broccoli
______ a pepper
______ a tomato

**C** Carbohydrates

______ bread
______ a cake
______ crackers
______ pasta
______ potatoes
______ rice

**D** Proteins

______ cheese
______ chicken
______ eggs
______ fish
______ meat
______ seafood

**2 Work with a partner. Cover the words and look at the pictures. Ask and answer questions.**

What's this?
A mango.
What are these?
Grapes.

## Focus on prepositions of place

**1 Match the pictures with the sentences about the key.**

______ It's **on** the wall.
______ It's **in** the lock.
______ It's **on** the table.
______ It's **under** the rock.
______ It's **above** the heart.
______ It's **next to** the plant.

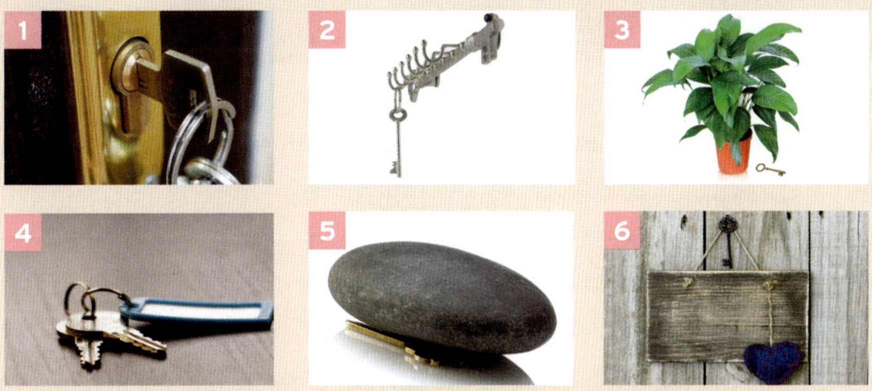

**2 Ask your partner questions about the classroom.**

Where's the clock?
It's on the wall above the door.

# 8 Money

## READING

**1** 2.11 **Read the article about Frankie. Who did Frankie want to help?**

charitystories.com

*charitystories.com* Home **Blog** Donate Contact search

# A Charity Haircut

Frankie was very excited to go to New York to see a show on Broadway with her parents. They had a big dinner in a fancy restaurant, more expensive than usual, and went to the theater. After the show, Frankie saw a homeless man. She was really upset to see this, so she bought him some cookies. The man was happy, but Frankie was happier. She liked to help people. And she wanted to do more.

Frankie always saved her Christmas money. But this wasn't enough money to make a difference. So, with the help of Mom's credit card, she created a page on the internet to collect money. Then, Frankie asked people to send money for the homeless. If the total was over $500, she promised to cut off her hair. But people donated more – a lot more. When she cut her hair, the total was $2,500!

Frankie's hair was shorter, but she liked it. She donated all the money to a homeless charity to help pay their bills. But she doesn't want to stop. "I want to help children's charities now."

**2 Are these sentences about Frankie true or false?**

**a** Frankie saw a show about Broadway. *False*

**b** She bought dinner for a homeless man.

**c** Frankie bought cookies with her mom's credit card.

**d** She had a haircut.

**e** She raised $2,500.

**f** She doesn't want to help any more people.

**3 Put the following items in the correct order to make a summary of the article.**

**a** to see a show. She saw a [2]

**b** give some money. Frankie created [ ]

**c** raised $2,500 for having [ ]

**d** a hair cut. Frankie gave the [ ]

**e** She went to New York [1]

**f** homeless man. She decided to [ ]

**g** money to charity. [ ]

**h** an internet page. She [ ]

2.12 **Listen and check.**

- **Grammar:** Comparative & superlative adjectives
- **Vocabulary:** Money. Big numbers.
- **Language for Life:** Describing objects

## VOCABULARY

**1 Complete each sentence with a word from the article on page 58.**

a I *bought* some new clothes last weekend. (line 3)
b I never ____________ money. I always spend all my money. (line 5)
c I never use my ____________ card to buy things online. (line 6)
d I ____________ money to charity once a year. (line 9)
e I always pay my ____________ on time. (line 11)

2.13 **Listen, check, and repeat.**

**2 Check (✓) the sentences in Exercise 1 that are true for you. Compare with a partner.**

## GRAMMAR

**1 Underline the comparative adjectives in the sentences.**

a They had a big dinner in a fancy restaurant, more expensive than usual, and went to the theater.
b The man was happy, but Frankie was happier.
c Frankie's hair was shorter, but she liked it.

### Comparative adjectives

**Short adjectives: + *er***
cheap → cheap**er**
nice → nice**r**
big → big**ger**
lucky → luck**ier**

**Long adjectives: *more* + adjective**
careful → **more** careful
beautiful → **more** beautiful

**Irregular forms**
good → better
bad → worse
far → farther

**2 Complete the table with comparative forms of the adjectives in the box.**

~~beautiful~~ big clean fast good happy important old rich

| Short adjectives (+ *er*) | Long adjectives (*more* + adjective) | Irregular forms |
|---|---|---|
| | *more beautiful* | |
| | | |
| | | |
| | | |
| | | |

2.14 **Listen, check, and repeat.**

**3 Write a list about things you'd like to have. Combine comparative adjectives from Exercise 2 with nouns in the box, or your own ideas.**

boyfriend/girlfriend a car a house a job

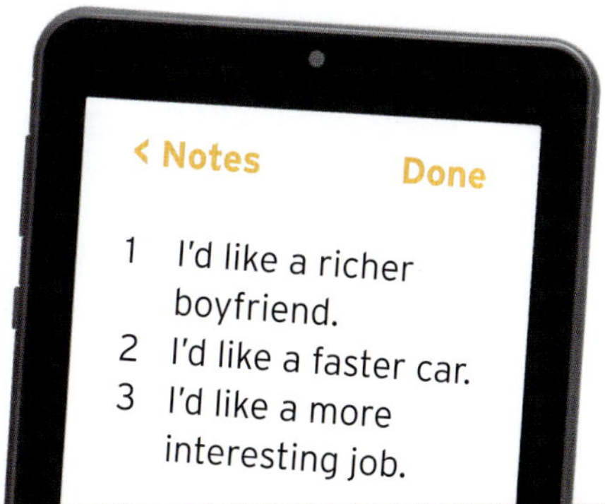


**Compare your sentences with a partner.**

**4 Work with a partner. Complete the sentences with the correct form of the adjective.**

a I'm *taller* than Karl. (tall)
b I'm ____________ than Terri. (old)
c My typing is ____________ than Gina's. (bad)
d My cell phone is ____________ than Eddie's. (small)
e My apartment is ____________ the office than Alan's. (far from)
f My computer was ____________ than Kerry's. (expensive)

2.15 **Listen, check, and repeat.**

**5 Replace the names in Exercise 4 with the names of people in the class or people you know. Make true sentences.**

## PRONUNCIATION

1 2.16 **Listen and repeat the chants.**

**A**
I'm taller than my sister.
I'm taller than my brother.
I'm taller than my mother.
I'm very, very tall!

**B**
I'm younger than my teacher.
I'm younger than my doctor.
I'm younger than my neighbor.
I'm very, very young!

2 **Which lines in the chants are true for you?**

## VOCABULARY & LISTENING

1 **Write the prices in full.**

a $1,250,620 *One million, two hundred and fifty thousand, six hundred and twenty dollars*
b $612,000 ______
c $3,877,180 ______
d $65,208 ______

2.17 **Listen, check, and repeat.**

2 **Work with a partner. Match the things (1-4) with the prices (a-d) in Exercise 1.**

1

2

3

4

2.18 **Listen and check.**

## SPEAKING

1 **What is your most valuable possession? Tell your partner.**

My most valuable possession is my car.

2 **Write how much you usually pay for the following things.**

a a pair of shoes
b a pair of jeans
c a jacket or overcoat
d a gift for a friend
e dinner in a restaurant
f a haircut

3 **Compare your answers with a partner.**

## GRAMMAR

**1 Complete the questions about your family with superlative adjectives.**

a Who's *the youngest*? (young)
b Who's ____________? (old)
c Who's ____________? (interesting)
d Who's ____________? (lucky)
e Who's ____________? (bad driver)
f Who's ____________? (good cook)

2.19 **Listen, check, and repeat.**

**2 Work with a partner. Ask and answer the questions in Exercise 1 about your family.**

Who's the youngest person in your family?

My niece, Teresa. She's five months old.

**Superlative adjectives**

**Short adjectives: *the + est***

young → the young**est**
nice → the nic**est**
bi**g** → the big**gest**
ugl**y** → the ugl**iest**

**Long adjectives: *the most* + adjective**

famous → **the most** famous
expensive → **the most** expensive

**Irregular forms**

good → the best
bad → the worst

3 **Pairwork Student A:** page 98 **Student B:** page 102

4 **Grammar Extra 8** page 108. Read the explanation and do the exercises.

## READING

**1 Look at the objects. In your opinion, which are the most common things to lose?**

a 
b 
c 
d 
e 
f 
g 
h 

**2** 2.20 **Read the article and check your ideas.**

# Lost On The Tube

by Sal McDonald
RealNews
21 April

**We're in the lost property office at Baker Street station in London. This office is now over 80 years old and it collects items left on the Tube, London's subway system.**

Did you leave your umbrella on the train? Well, don't worry. It's here. With 10,907 other umbrellas – this is the total number of lost umbrellas in London in just one year! We're in the lost property office at Baker Street station in London. This office is now over 80 years old and it collects items left on the Tube, London's subway system.

Umbrellas are the most common thing to lose. But what are some of the other things people leave behind?

Well, some people forget their false teeth. And a couple of people lost their artificial legs! Somebody even left their wedding dress on the train – they didn't find the owner.

People forget or drop many things. Keys, of course, money, purses, glasses, even a few passports. And teddy bears! Children leave two hundred bears on the trains every year. But don't worry – the bears go to a good home at Christmas. The lost property office gives them to charity.

**3 Work in small groups. Discuss the questions.**

a Which things from Exercise 1 do you have with you now/at home/at work or school?
b Which things do you often/sometimes/never lose?
c When was the last time you lost something? What happened? Where did you find it?

## LANGUAGE FOR LIFE

1 ▶ 2.21 **Read and listen to Judy's conversation with a lost property clerk. Answer the questions.**

a Which bag (1-3) did Judy lose?

b What was in Judy's bag?

1 

2 

3 

**Clerk:** Lost property. Can I help you?
**Judy:** Good morning. I'm calling because I lost my bag yesterday.
**Clerk:** I see. Well, there are thirty-eight bags here. What color is it and what's it made of?
**Judy:** It's black and it's made of leather.
**Clerk:** Hm ... black ... leather ...
There are twenty-four black leather bags here.
So what kind of bag is it?
**Judy:** It's a purse. A small purse.
**Clerk:** Is there anything in it?
**Judy:** Yes, there's a cell phone and some glasses. Oh, and Hissy.
**Clerk:** Hissy?
**Judy:** Yes, Hissy the snake.
**Clerk:** There's a snake ... in your purse?
**Judy:** Yes, but don't worry, it's made of plastic.
It belongs to my five-year-old son.
**Clerk:** OK, well, I think we have your purse here.
The office is open from nine in the morning until ...

2 **Match the questions with possible answers. Underline the answers Judy gives in the conversation.**

| | | | |
|---|---|---|---|
| a | What color is it? | 1 | It's a **backpack** / **tote bag** / **purse**. |
| b | What's it made of? | 2 | It's **black** / **red** / **white**. |
| c | What kind of bag is it? | 3 | There's a **passport** / **pen** / **plastic snake**. |
| d | Is there anything in it? | 4 | It's made of **leather** / **plastic** / **cotton**. |

▶ 2.22 **Listen, check, and repeat the expressions.**

3 **Work with a partner. Imagine you lost your own bag. Write a conversation between you and a lost property clerk. Practice the conversation.**

### Life Skills: Comparing Products

A New Phone

1 **Read the two reviews. Complete using the words from the box.**

~~money~~ save cash credit

zoopa.com

ZOOPA.COM Home Shop Compare Contact search

**GRu15 Smartphone**

a 
*****

This phone is amazing! It's the best phone ever! So much better than my old phone. It has better apps, a nicer screen, and the camera takes the most amazing photos. It's great value for (1) __money__. Buy it now and you can (2) __________ 15%.

*published 5 days ago by timandeve*

b 
*****

This is the worst phone. It's more expensive than other phones, but it isn't better. It's slower than the GrU13 and the screen is smaller. I'm glad I used my (3) __________ card so I can get my money back. Save your (4) __________ and buy something else.

*published 8 days ago by sally2020*

▶ 2.23 **Listen and check.**

2 **List the good and bad qualities of the phone according to the reviewers.**

3 **Work with a partner. Compare your own phone to the Gru15. Which phone is better?**

My phone is smaller than the Gru15 ...

MACMILLAN LIFE SKILLS

# 8 Vocabulary Extra

## Common adjectives

**1 Match the pictures with the adjectives.**

| | | | |
|---|---|---|---|
| 10 big | ____ dirty | ____ happy | ____ rich |
| ____ boring | ____ early | ____ long | ____ ugly |
| ____ cheap | ____ fast | ____ loud | ____ young |
| ____ difficult | ____ good | ____ lucky | |

**2 Match the adjectives in the box with their opposites in Exercise 1.**

*bad – good*

~~bad~~ beautiful clean easy expensive interesting late
old poor quiet sad short slow small unlucky

**3 Work with a partner. Ask and answer questions.**

What's the opposite of dirty?

Clean. What's the opposite of poor?

## Focus on *like*

**1 Complete the table with the phrases in the box.**

~~Do you like sushi?~~ I don't like doing the dishes.
She doesn't like him. They'd like a vacation. They like cooking.

| Some uses of *like* | Examples | | | |
|---|---|---|---|---|
| **a** *like* + noun = ☺ | I really like dance music. | I don't like it. | (1) *Do you like sushi?* | (2) ____ |
| **b** *like + ing* = enjoy an activity | We like sailing. | He likes going out. | (3) ____ | (4) ____ |
| **c** *would like* + noun = want something | I'd like a chicken sandwich. | Would you like a drink? | (5) ____ | |

**2 Write your own example sentence for each use of *like*.**

# 9 Talent

## LISTENING

1 **Work with a partner. Match the pictures (1-4) with the names. What do you know about these famous people?**

Justin Bieber ☐ Taylor Swift ☐ Shakira ☐ Colin Farrell ☐

1

2

3
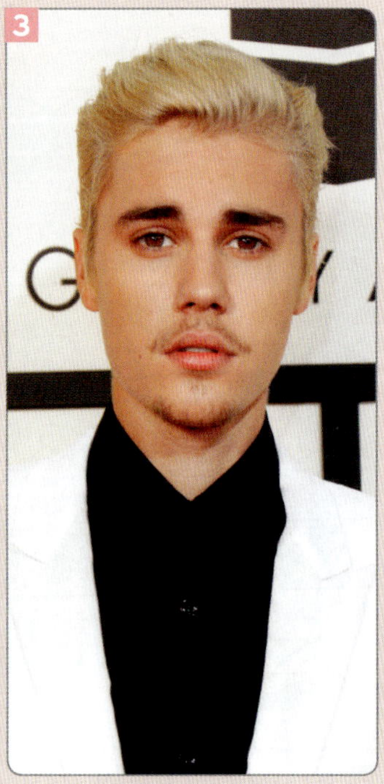

4

2 **You are going to listen to a podcast called *Celebrity Secrets*. Guess which famous person from Exercise 1 can do the following things.**

a ________________ can make jam.
b ________________ can complete a Rubik's cube.
c ________________ can line dance.
d ________________ can speak five languages.

▶ 2.24 **Listen and check your ideas.**

## GRAMMAR

1 **Complete the questions and answers.**

a Can you make jam? Yes, I can. No, I can't.
b Can your father dance? Yes, he ______. No, he ______.
c ______ you swim? ______. ______.
d ______ you speak five languages? ______. ______.
e ______ your mother ride a horse? ______. ______.
f ______ your parents ski? ______. ______.

▶ 2.25 **Listen, check, and repeat.**

> ***can/can't***
>
> **Can** you play poker?
> Yes, I **can**.
> No, I **can't**.
> (can**'t** = can**not**)

2 **Work with a partner. Ask and answer the questions in Exercise 1.**

3 **Grammar Extra 9** page 110. Read the explanation and do the exercises.

- **Grammar:** *can* (for ability). Adverbs of manner. Frequency expressions.
- **Vocabulary:** Character adjectives
- **Language for Life:** Making excuses

## PRONUNCIATION

**1** 2.26 **Listen and repeat the chants. Notice the stress.**

**A**
I can ski, I can swim,
I can dance, I can sing.
What can you do?
What can you do?

**B**
Can she ski? Can she swim?
Can she dance? Can she sing?
Yes, she can.
Yes, she can.

**C**
He can't ski. He can't swim.
He can't dance. He can't sing.
No, he can't.
No, he can't.

**2** **In which chant(s) is *can/can't* stressed? In which chant(s) is *can/can't* not stressed?**

**Practice the chants in Exercise 1.**

## GRAMMAR

**1** **Complete each sentence with a verb phrase from the box or your own ideas.**

I can drive very well.

I can play the piano pretty well.

I can't cook very well.

**Adverbs of manner**

**Adjective + *ly***
slow → slow**ly**
careful → careful**ly**
happy → happi**ly**

**Irregular forms**
good → well
fast → fast

cook dance draw drive play soccer play the piano sing ski swim

**a** I can ________ very well. **b** I can ________ pretty well. **c** I can't ________ very well.

**2** **Match the adjectives with the corresponding adverbs.**

| Adjective | Adverb |
|---|---|
| bad | loudly |
| careful | slowly |
| fast | badly |
| good | happily |
| happy | fast |
| loud | quietly |
| quiet | well |
| slow | carefully |

**Answer the questions.**

**a** How do you form most adverbs?
**b** Which adverbs are irregular?

**3** **Put the words in the correct order.**

**a** I / very slowly / eat / my food

| **subject** + | **verb** + | **object** | **+ adverb** |
|---|---|---|---|
| *I* | *eat* | *my food* | *very slowly.* |

**b** I / drive / pretty fast / my car
**c** I / play / very badly / the guitar
**d** I / my money / spend / very carefully
**e** I / very loudly / the drums / play
**f** I / don't eat / very quietly / my soup
**g** I / very happily / do / my homework
**h** I / don't speak / very well / English

2.27 **Listen, check, and repeat.**

**How many sentences are true for you? Compare with a partner.**

## READING

1 **How many famous dancers do you know? Discuss with a partner.**

2 2.28 **Read the article about Misty Copeland. Complete the headings with the words in the box.**

| ~~Early life~~ | Writing | Success | Meals | Sleep | Travel | Free time |
|---|---|---|---|---|---|---|

# Fun Facts: Misty Copeland

**a** Early life

Misty Copeland was born in Kansas City, USA, and grew up in California. Her mother was a Kansas City Chiefs cheerleader. Misty didn't go to ballet classes when she was a child because her mother worked sixty hours a week. She started studying dance at 13 years old.

**b** ______

In 2000, Misty joined the American Ballet Theater Studio. She studied every day. Her dancing got better and better. In 2007, she was the first African-American woman to give a solo performance.

**c** ______

Now a famous dancer, Misty practices eight hours a day. In her free time, Misty loves to cook and relax. On Sundays, she spends time with her husband and family.

**d** ______

Misty is not just a great dancer - she's also a best-selling writer! She wrote a book about her life, *Life in Motion*, and it was a big hit. She also wrote a children's book, *Firebird*. She wants to publish a new book every two years.

**e** ______

Misty has to eat healthy food. She eats nuts and dried fruits three times a day. She has something light for lunch, like sushi. Misty doesn't eat meat, so she usually eats seafood for dinner.

**f** ______

Misty travels a lot. Every month she dances in a different theater across the country. Misty is an inspiration to girls everywhere and she loves meeting her fans.

**g** ______

Misty needs to have energy and strength to be a good dancer. She knows that sleep is very important. Wherever she is, Misty always sleeps for 8 hours a night.

3 **Match the beginnings and the endings of these sentences according to the article.**

| | |
|---|---|
| **a** She travels | eight hours a night. |
| **b** She sleeps | three times a day. |
| **c** She practices | sixty hours a week. |
| **d** She eats nuts | every month. |
| **e** She wants to publish a book | eight hours a day. |
| **f** Her mother worked | every two years. |

2.29 **Listen and check.**

## GRAMMAR

1 **Number the expressions in the box in order of frequency, from *Frequent* (1) to *Not frequent* (6).**

every two weeks ___ every day ___ four times a year 6
once a month ___ three times a day 1 twice a week ___

2.30 **Listen, check, and repeat.**

2 **Complete the questions with the missing word in the correct place.**

**a** How often you travel? (do) How often do you travel?

**b** How do you buy new shoes? (often)

**c** How often do call your family? (you)

2.31 **Listen, check, and repeat.**

**Ask your partner the questions**

3 **Pairwork** **Student A:** page 98 **Student B:** page 102

**Frequency expressions**

**Frequent**
- all the time
- once a day
- every week
- twice a month
- every year
- every four years
- never

**Not frequent**

## VOCABULARY

1 **Match the adjectives with the meanings.**

a confident
b generous
c selfish
d sensible
e serious
f shy

1 You give a lot of time and/or money to people.
2 You are nervous about meeting people.
3 You are very sure of yourself.
4 You think about things and don't laugh much.
5 You don't think about other people.
6 You never do stupid things.

2.32 **Listen and check.**

**Which adjective always has a negative meaning?**

2 **Which three adjectives best describe you? Use adjectives from Exercise 1 or your own ideas. Compare with a partner.**

## READING

1 2.33 **Read the comments. Are you (or a friend) like one of these people? Discuss with a partner.**

goodreads.com

Good reads

Home Latest stories News search

# Not Rude, Just Shy?

a **Eva**
What a great blog. People think I'm being rude or selfish if I don't talk to them. But I'm just very, very shy. I often hide behind my hair! I was so glad to read this – other people feel the same way as me! Yay!
reply · like · follow *May 12 at 10:41 p.m.*

b **Steve**
Thank you for this blog! I always thought my co-worker was just really serious and boring. Now I understand! She is just shy! I'm going to talk to her again. I know I'm very confident, but I need to understand other people are less confident.
reply · like · follow *May 12 at 9:45 p.m.*

c **Patrick**
I'm quite shy when I meet people I don't know. I'm not very good at making small talk! I never know what to say. This blog makes me feel better. I always think everyone is more confident and friendly than me, but maybe it's not true. Maybe we are all a little shy.
reply · like · follow *May 11 at 7:32 p.m.*

2 **Write descriptions of three people you know well. Begin with *People think* ...**

People think my aunt Mary is friendly and generous.

## LANGUAGE FOR LIFE

**1 Match the top six excuses for not doing exercise (a-f) with the pictures (1-6).**

a I have a bad back. 2
b I don't have time. ___
c I'm really tired. ___
d I have a cold. ___
e I have a headache. ___
f I don't have any money. ___

2.34 **Listen, check, and repeat.**

**2** 2.35 **Read and listen to the conversation. Check (✓) the excuses in Exercise 1 that Lisa uses.**

**Dan:** Do you want to go to the gym later?
**Lisa:** Oh, no, I can't. I'm really tired.
**Dan:** What about tomorrow?
**Lisa:** No, I can't. I have a bad back.
**Dan:** You should go swimming – swimming is really good for your back.
**Lisa:** I can't go swimming, I have a cold.
**Dan:** Oh, no. Well, you should have a massage.
**Lisa:** I can't, I don't have any money.
**Dan:** Do you want to go for a walk on Sunday?
**Lisa:** No, I can't.
**Dan:** Don't tell me – you have a bad foot.
**Lisa:** No, I can't go for a walk because I'm going shopping.
**Dan:** But you don't have any money.
**Lisa:** What?
**Dan:** Nothing.

**3** 2.36 **Listen and repeat the expressions.**

a Do you want to go to the gym?
b No, I can't.
c I'm really tired.
d What about tomorrow?
e I have a bad back.
f You should go swimming.

**4 Work with a partner. Write a similar conversation to the one in Exercise 2. Use your favorite excuse for not doing exercise.**

**Practice the conversation.**

### Life Skills: Criticizing

Polite or Rude?

**1** 2.37 **Listen and match the conversations (1-3) and the pictures (a-c).**

1 ☐ 2 ☐ 3 ☐

**2 Look at these statements. Write P for polite comments and write R for a rude comment.**

a I think you can do better. P
b You are terrible! ______
c Good try. ______
d You can't sing! ______
e She can't speak English very well. ______
f You're doing really well. ______

**3 Work with a partner. Make comments on these situations.**

He's not playing very well.

MACMILLAN LIFE SKILLS

# 9 Vocabulary Extra

## Common adverbs

**1 Match the pictures with the sentences.**

__3__ She's driving carefully.
_______ He's winning easily.
_______ She's typing fast.
_______ They're playing happily.
_______ He's working hard.
_______ He's laughing loudly.
_______ She's reading quietly.
_______ He's speaking slowly.
_______ She's singing well.

**2 Work with a partner. Cover the sentences and look at the pictures. Ask and answer questions.**

What's he doing?

He's working hard.
What's she doing?

## Focus on *be*

**1 Complete the table with the phrases in the box.**

Be careful! He's twenty-one. I'm cold. ~~She's an architect.~~
There are some new students. They're bored. We're waiting for a bus.

| Some uses of be | Examples | | | |
|---|---|---|---|---|
| a *be* + *a/an* + job | I'm a teacher. | He's a doctor. | (1) She's an architect. | |
| b *be* + age*/height | I'm forty-six. | She is 1 meter 68. | (2) ________ | |
| c *be* + feelings/ physical states** | She's happy. | We're thirsty. | (3) ________ | (4) ________ |
| d *be* + adjectives = imperative | Be quiet! | Don't be stupid! | (5) ________ | |
| e *there* + *be* = something exists | There's a message. | There aren't any tickets. | (6) ________ | |
| f *be* + *ing* = present progressive | I'm just looking. | She's wearing a suit. | (7) ________ | |

***Note:** To talk about age, you use *be* (not *have*):
***I'm** twenty-three.* (NOT ~~*I have twenty-three.*~~)

****Note:** To talk about physical states, you use *be* (not *have*): ***I'm** hungry*. (NOT ~~*I have hunger.*~~)

**2 Write your own example sentences for each use of *be*.**

# Review C

## GRAMMAR

**Grammar Extra** pages 108 and 110.

**1 Write four countable nouns and four uncountable nouns in the table.**

a apples

b meat

c strawberries

d milk

e bananas

f water

g bread

h eggs

| | | | | |
|---|---|---|---|---|
| **Countable** | *apples* | | | |
| **Uncountable** | *meat* | | | |

**2 Look at the pictures in Exercise 1 and complete the conversation. Use the words in the box.**

~~Are~~ are is is isn't lot many much

**Marie:** (1) *Are* there any eggs?
**Tom:** Yes, there (2) ________.
**Marie:** How (3) ________?
**Tom:** A (4) ________.

**Marie:** And (5) ________ there any milk?
**Tom:** Yes, there (6) ________.
**Marie:** How (7) ________?
**Tom:** There (8) ________ much.

**3 Write the questions in the correct order.**

a you / swim / can ? *Can you swim?*
b ski / can / you ?
c you / can / the guitar / play ?
d a motorcycle / you / ride / can ?
e drive / a bus / can / you ?
f you / three languages / can / speak ?

**4 Write the adverbs.**

a bad *badly*
b careful
c fast
d good
e happy
f loud
g quiet
h slow

**5 Write the comparative or superlative form of each adjective.**

a Who's the (young) *youngest* man in the class?
b Buenos Aires is a (nice) __________ city than London.
c Who's the (tall) __________ woman in the class?
d Soccer is (interesting) __________ than golf.
e Clothes are (cheap) __________ in New York than in Paris.
f Who has the (beautiful) __________ smile in the class?
g Who's wearing the (interesting) __________ clothes in the class?

**6 Find the mistake! Cross out the incorrect sentence.**

1 a ~~Jake is the best student than Monica.~~
  b Jake is a better student than Monica.
2 a Who has the most good car?
  b Who has the best car?
3 a I can playing the piano.
  b I can play the piano.
4 a He drives very fast.
  b He very fast drives.
5 a Is there any cheese?
  b Are there any cheese?
6 a I'm the happiest person in the world!
  b I'm the most happiest person in the world!

## VOCABULARY

1 **Read the clues and find the names of the types of food.**

apple banana bread carrot cheese egg fish orange ~~pasta~~ potato rice

a Italy's favorite carbohydrate. *pasta*
b A red or green fruit.
c A long, yellow fruit.
d You make sandwiches with this carbohydrate.
e You make French fries with this.
f Asia's favorite carbohydrate.
g An orange vegetable.
h This form of protein makes an omelet.
i A form of protein from the ocean.
j A form of protein from milk.
k A round, orange fruit.

2 **Match the amounts of money in numbers (a-e) with the amounts in words (1-5). Practice saying the amounts.**

a $1,100
b $11,100
c $1,100,000
d $11,100,000
e $111,100,000

1 one million, one hundred thousand dollars
2 eleven million, one hundred thousand dollars
3 one thousand, one hundred dollars
4 one hundred and eleven million, one hundred thousand dollars
5 eleven thousand, one hundred dollars

3 **Look at the pictures and complete the sentences. Transform the adjectives into adverbs.**

a 
fast

b 
bad

c 
hard

d 
quiet

e 
loud

f 
slow

a He drives very *fast*.
b She sings very ______.
c He works ______.
d She's speaking very ______.
e They're laughing very ______.
f He types very ______.

4 **Underline the correct word.**

a Tom is very sure of himself. He's really **generous** / **confident**.
b Carly's very **serious** / **sensible**. She never does stupid things, but she loves to laugh.
c Alan's nervous about meeting my parents. He's very **shy** / **selfish**.
d Joel's so **confident** / **generous**. He buys presents for everyone.
e Katy never thinks about other people – she's so **selfish** / **sensible**.
f Rhonda's very **serious** / **shy**. She thinks about things a lot and she never smiles.

**Work with a partner. Choose two adjectives to describe your partner. Ask your partner to guess which adjectives you chose.**

## PRONUNCIATION

1 **Look at some words from Units 7-9. Say the words and add them to the table.**

~~banana~~ ~~carefully~~ ~~lemon~~ potato sandwiches badly happily strawberries boring tomato

| | |
|---|---|
| A: ■ ▪ | *lemon* |
| B: ■ ▪ ▪ | *carefully* |
| C: ▪ ■ ▪ | *banana* |

2 **Underline the stressed syllable in each word.**

2.38 **Listen, check, and repeat.**

## READING & LISTENING

**1** 2.39 **Read the descriptions of three restaurants. Are the sentences true or false?**

a The Steak Shop is one of the best seafood restaurants. *False*
b The Steak Shop serves awesome desserts.
c Inamo is a cheap Japanese restaurant.
d Inamo only serves seafood.
e Luigi's was in ***The Godfather*** movie.
f Luigi's has very fresh bread.

bookymytable.net

**book my table** Home Book a Table Reviews search

### The Steak Shop
**** 351 reviews
94% recommended
$$$
Midtown
American

**What:** This is one of the best restaurants in Midtown. The Steak Shop promises to cook your steak perfectly. They also serve freshly cooked bread, delicious salads, and awesome cakes. The wine list is long but it's not cheap.
**Who:** For the well-dressed meat eater.
**When:** Lunch menu, reservations recommended for dinner

### Inamo
**** 223 reviews
86% recommended
$$$$
Midtown
Japanese

**What:** For the freshest fish, delicious soups, and the best view, Inamo is a great choice in Midtown. It serves traditional Japanese food. But if you are not a fan of sushi, you can try the chicken curry and rice. It's very nice, and very expensive!
**Who:** For the fish lover.
**When:** Only open for dinner

### Luigi's
*** 756 reviews
73% recommended
$$$
Midtown
Italian

**What:** Imagine you are in *The Godfather* at Luigi's in Midtown! Luigi's has hot bread, HUGE bowls of pasta, and cheap red wines. The chicken and seafood are not bad. It's perfect for a long, slow, and delicious Italian meal.
**Who:** For the Robert De Niro fan.
**When:** Cheaper for lunch after 1:30 p.m.

**2 Work with a partner. Choose one of the restaurants in Exercise 1 for these people. Say why you chose it.**

a Someone who loves gangster movies.
b Someone who likes fresh fish.
c Someone who drinks expensive wine.

**3** 2.40 **Listen to the telephone conversation and complete the information about Lara's reservation.**

**RESERVATION**
Lunch or dinner: (1) *Dinner*
Date: (2) ____________
Number of people: (3) ____________
Time: (4) ____________
Name: (5) ____________

**4 Underline the correct answers.**

a There aren't any tables for **lunch** / **dinner** on Friday.
b It's Lara's birthday on **Friday** / **Saturday**.
c There **are some** / **aren't any** window tables for dinner on Saturday.
d You **can** / **can't** see the park from the restaurant.
e Dress at the restaurant is **casual** / **formal**.
f The restaurant **takes** / **doesn't take** credit cards.

## WRITING & SPEAKING

1 **Read the email. How does Patricia start and end the email?**

mail.com

**mail.com**

Compose
Inbox
Drafts
Sent
Spam
Trash

**Patricia** <patriciad@bmail.com> 10:54 a.m. (2 hours ago)
to <daviesfamily@bmail.com>

Dear Mom and Dad

**1**
Just a short message from paradise! It's lovely here. We're staying at the Palm Beach Hotel. It's amazing. Our room is huge, and there's a big TV in our bathroom! The shower is outside, under the trees.

**2**
The place is really relaxing, and it's easy to walk around the island. I'm not sure I want to leave. There aren't any cars on the island. It's really quiet. And there aren't many people at the hotel, so we're very lucky.

**3**
Every day, we can go for an early morning swim. And there are so many water sports. We can dive before lunch, and then we can surf in the afternoon. I can surf … and Ian can fall off the board very well!

**4**
Yesterday, we went to a market in a village. Then we ate at a fantastic restaurant on the beach. The fruit was delicious. We're having a great time!

See you soon!

Love,
Patricia

2 **Read the email again. Which paragraph describes these things? Write the paragraph number.**

a Where Patricia is staying.
b What she can do there.
c What she did yesterday.
d What the place is like.

3 **Make a list of all the adjectives Patricia uses in the email.**

4 **Work with a partner. Imagine you are on a vacation now. Ask and answer questions about your vacation.**

a Where / you?
b What / the place / like?
c What / can / do?
d What do / every day?
e What / do yesterday?

**Is your vacation similar to your partner's?**

5 **Write an email about the vacation you imagined in Exercise 4. Write four paragraphs. Use adjectives to describe your vacation.**

# 10 TV

## VOCABULARY

**1 Complete the sentences with the words in the box.**

channels   on   show   turn on   ~~TVs~~   watch

a How many ____TVs____ do you have in your house?
b How many hours of TV do you ________ every day?
c When do you usually ________ the TV? When do you turn it off?
d How many different ________ can you get on your TV?
e What's your favorite TV ________?
f What's ________ TV this evening?

2.41 **Listen, check, and repeat.**

**2 Work with a partner. Ask and answer the questions in Exercise 1.**

**3** 2.42 **Listen and number (1-6) the TV shows in the order you hear them.**

a game show ____1____

a documentary ________

the news ________

a soap opera ________

a reality TV show ________

a talk show ________

**4 Write down the names of some TV shows in your country. What kinds of shows are they?**

## SPEAKING

**1 Work in small groups. Discuss the questions.**

a What TV shows do you often watch / sometimes watch / never watch?
b Right now, which show(s) do you really like / really hate?
c Which TV channel has the best shows / the worst shows?

- **Grammar:** Future forms: *want to, would like to, hope to, going to*
- **Vocabulary:** TV shows
- **Language for Life:** Suggestions and offers

## READING & LISTENING

1 2.43 **Read the *Who's Got Talent?* homepage and answer the questions.**

a What kind of person do they want on *Who's Got Talent*?
b What is the top prize?

whosgottalent.com

### Who's Got Talent?

How about you?

We're looking for new contestants for the nation's No.1 TV show!
- Are you a confident performer with real talent?
- Are you a singer? A dancer? A magician?
- Do you want to be on the *Who's Got Talent?* stage?
- Would you like to win $1 million and join the *Who's Got Talent?* nationwide tour?

**Email or text us and answer this one simple question: Why do you want to be on *Who's Got Talent?***

2 2.44 **Listen and read. Match the people (a-e) with the reasons (1-5) they give to be on *Who's Got Talent?***

1 I hope to win *#whosgottalent*? because my sister is in the hospital. I want to pay her medical bills. [a]
2 We'd like to win the $1 million prize money and buy new outfits and shoes. [ ]
3 I want to go on *#whosgottalent*? because I want to show people I'm a funny guy! [ ]
4 I'd like to save the planet! I'd like to win the money and give it to Greenpeace. [ ]
5 I hope to get a recording contract and money to buy my mom a new house. [ ]

**Discuss with a partner. Which contestant gives the best reason? Which contestant gives the worst reason?**

## GRAMMAR

1 **Look again at Exercise 2. Underline the verb structures *hope*, *want*, and *'d like (would like)*.**

a Do these verb structures refer to the past or the future?
b Are *hope*, *want*, and *'d like* followed by the infinitive with *to*, or the infinitive without *to*?

2 **Put the words in the correct order.**

a I / travel / to/ around the world / want
I want to travel around the world.
b want / live / to / in a different country / I
c a lot of children / like / have / I'd / to
d be famous / to / wouldn't / I / like
e hope / before I'm sixty / I / retire / to

2.45 **Listen, check, and repeat.**

**Check (✓) the sentences that are true for you. Compare with a partner.**

## LISTENING & READING

1 2.46 **Read and listen to an interview with Lola, the winner of *Who's Got Talent*? She's talking about her future plans. What would she like to do?**

**Interviewer:** Lola, congratulations!
**Lola:** Thanks! I can't believe it!
**Interviewer:** What's the first thing (1) _you're going to_ do now you have won *Who's Got Talent*?
**Lola:** (2) ____________ have a big party! I want to thank all my family and friends.
**Interviewer:** Ah. What (3) ____________ do with the money?
**Lola:** (4) ____________ buy a house for my mom
**Interviewer:** Oh, that's great. Which of the *Who's Got Talent?* finalists (5) ____________ see again?
**Lola:** There are some people I'd like to see again, but (6) ____________ see Josh or Sammy – they were mean to me.
**Interviewer:** Oh, that's a shame ... But what about Eddie? You became really good friends on the show. (7) ____________ see Eddie again?
**Lola:** Yes, of course (8) ____________ see each other. I miss him already!
**Interviewer:** Finally, Lola, what are your plans for the future?
**Lola:** Well, first (9) ____________ go out and spend some money. Then I want to start my singing career. (10) ____________ record some songs. I'd also like to go on tour.
**Interviewer:** Oh, well, good luck!

2 **Complete the conversation in Exercise 1 with the correct form of *going to*. Listen again and check your answers.**

## GRAMMAR

1 **Complete the questions and answers about Lola's future.**

| | | | |
|---|---|---|---|
| a | _Is_ she going to have a big party? | Yes, _she is_. | No, _she isn't_. |
| b | _____ she going to buy a house for her mom? | Yes, _she_ _____. | No, _she_ _____. |
| c | _____ going to see Josh and Sammy? | Yes, _____. | No, _____. |
| d | _____ to see Eddie? | _____. | _____. |
| e | _____ go out and spend some money? | _____. | _____. |
| f | _____ record some songs? | _____. | _____. |

2.47 **Listen, check, and repeat.**

2 **Work with a partner. Ask and answer the questions in Exercise 1.**

3 **Rewrite these good intentions with the missing word in the correct place.**

a I'm going do more sports. (to) *I'm going to do more sports.*
b I going to eat healthier food. ('m)
c I going to save more money. ('m)
d I'm going spend more time with my family. (to)
e I not going to watch so much TV. ('m)
f I'm going to arrive late for appointments. (not)

4 **Which of the good intentions in Exercise 3 do you have? Discuss with a partner.**

5 **Grammar Extra 10** page 110. Read the explanation and do the exercises.

**(be) going to**

| | | |
|---|---|---|
| I**'m** | | |
| You**'re** | | |
| He**'s** | | be. |
| She**'s** | **going to** | come. |
| It**'s** | | work. |
| We**'re** | | |
| They**'re** | | |

**Are** you **going to come**?
Yes, I **am**.
No, I**'m not**.

## GRAMMAR

1 **Ask your partner questions about their future plans and intentions.**

| Question | | Answer |
|---|---|---|
| What are you going to do | after class? | |
| | this evening? | *I'm going to …* |
| | tomorrow? | |
| | next weekend? | *I don't know.* |
| | next summer? | |

What are you going to do after class?

I'm going to meet my friend for a drink.

2 **Pairwork** **Student A:** page 99 **Student B:** page 103

## PRONUNCIATION

1 2.48 **Listen and repeat the chants. What is the missing word? How do you pronounce it in the chants?**

**A**

What do you want ____________ do?
Where do you want ____________ go?
Who do you want ____________ see?
I don't want ____________ come.

**B**

What are you going ____________ do?
Where are you going ____________ go?
Who are you going ____________ see?
I'm not going ____________ come.

2 **Underline the stressed words in Exercise 1. Practice the chants.**

## SPEAKING: ANECDOTE

1 2.49 **Listen to Juliet talking about her favorite TV shows. Underline the correct information.**

a What's your favorite TV show? It's **Game of Thrones** / **The Big Bang Theory**.
b What kind of show is it? It's a **science show** / **comedy**.
c Who are the main characters? The main characters are **four men and one woman** / **five men**.
d What's it about? It's about **the characters' lives** / **general knowledge**.
e Who's your favorite character? I like **Raj** / **Penny**.
f What time is it on? It's on **Mondays at 8** / **Thursdays at 8**.
g What happened the last time you watched? **Raj moved into Leonard's apartment** / **Raj moved out of Leonard's apartment**.
h Why do you like it? I like **the humor** / **the fighting**.

2 **You're going to tell your partner about your favorite TV show.**

- Ask yourself the questions in Exercise 1.
- Think about *what* to say and *how* to say it.
- Tell your partner about your favorite TV show.

My favorite TV show is …

## LANGUAGE FOR LIFE

**1** 2.50 **Read and listen to the conversation. Who wants to watch *Pirates of the Caribbean*?**

**Ruby:** What's on TV tonight?
**Joe:** Nothing.
**Ruby:** Should we go out?
**Joe:** Good idea. (1) ____ go to the movies.
**Ruby:** (2) ____. What's playing?
**Joe:** I don't know.
**Ruby:** Just a minute – I'll look online. ... Oh, great. *Pirates of the Caribbean.*
**Joe:** What, again? It's so old.
**Ruby:** Should I book tickets?
**Joe:** (3) ____. I don't want to see it again. Let's stream a movie.
**Ruby:** OK. (4) ____ choose a movie?
**Joe:** No, it's OK – I'll choose. I'd like to see a movie without Johnny Depp in it.

**2 Complete the conversation with the words in the box.**

OK Let's No Should I

**Listen again and check.**

**3 Complete the table with phrases from the conversation in Exercise 1.**

| Make a suggestion | Agree | Offer to do something | Disagree |
|---|---|---|---|
| Should we ... | Good idea. | I'll ... | No, it's OK ... |

**4** 2.51 **Listen and repeat the expressions.**

a Should we go out?
b Good idea.
c Let's go to the movies.
d I'll look online.
e Should I book tickets?
f No, it's OK – I'll choose.

**Practice the conversation. Change the name of the movie and actor.**

### Life Skills: Being Creative
A New TV Show

**1** 2.52 **Listen to the descriptions of reality TV shows. Label the pictures using the titles in the box.**

Explorer Fire! Fire! Life With The Talbots Move! Get There First

a Explorer

b ____________

c ____________

d ____________

e ____________

**2 Think of a new reality TV show. Complete the table.**

| My Reality TV Show |
|---|
| Show name: ____________ |
| Show topic: ____________ |
| Stars of the show: ____________ |
| What happens: ____________ |

**3 Present your idea to a partner. Then decide which show is the best.**

MACMILLAN LIFE SKILLS

## GRAMMAR

1 2.62 **Read and listen to part of the conversation on page 82. Answer the questions.**

**Winnie:** Have you been to Brazil?
**Rick:** Yeah, I have.
**Winnie:** When did you go?
**Rick:** In February. I went to the Carnival in Rio.
**Winnie:** Awesome!

a What tense is the first question?
b What tense is the second question?
c Which tense do you use to focus on "when" something happened?

2 **Complete the simple past questions in the table.**

**Present perfect vs. simple past**

**Present perfect**
Completed action in "time up to now" (you *don't* focus on "when")

**Have** you **been** to Brazil?

Yes, I **have**.
No, I **haven't**.

**Simple past**
Completed action at a specific past time (you focus on "when")

When **did** you **go**?
I **went** in February.

| Present perfect | Simple past | |
|---|---|---|
| a Have you ever been to Cuba? | When / go?<br>When did you go? | Who / go with?<br>Who did you go with? |
| b Have you ever moved? | When / move? | Where / move to? |
| c Have you ever lost your credit card? | When / lose it? | What / do? |
| d Have you ever won a prize? | What / win? | When / win it? |
| e Have you ever seen a Tom Hanks movie? | When / see it? | Which one / see? |

2.63 **Listen, check, and repeat.**

3 **Ask your partner the questions (a-e) in Exercise 2. If they answer "yes," ask the follow-up questions in the simple past.**

4 **Grammar Extra 11** page 110. Read the explanation and do the exercises.

## SPEAKING: ANECDOTE

1 2.64 **Listen to Tom talking about his oldest friend. Underline the correct information.**

| | |
|---|---|
| a What's his or her name? | His name is **Bryan / Brett**. |
| b Where did you first meet? | We first met at **high school / college**. |
| c How old were you? | We were **eleven / fifteen or sixteen** years old. |
| d Why did you become friends? | **We like the same music / We laugh at the same things**. |
| e What does your friend do now? | He's **a doctor / a teacher**. |
| f How often do you see him? | I see him **all the time / a few times a year**. |
| g When was the last time you saw him? | **Last year / On his birthday**. |
| h What is your best memory of him? | **A vacation we took together / His wedding**. |

2 **You're going to tell your partner about your oldest friend.**

- Ask yourself the questions in Exercise 1.
- Think about *what* to say and *how* to say it.
- Tell your partner about your oldest friend.

My oldest friend is ...

## LANGUAGE FOR LIFE

**1 Read and put the parts (a-e) of the restaurant conversation in the correct order (1-5).**

1 *d* 2 ___ 3 ___ 4 ___ 5 ___

**a**
**Mrs. Jones:** Could we get the check, please?
**Server:** Sure. Was everything OK with your meal?
**Mrs. Jones:** Yes, it was great, thanks.

**b**
**Server:** Here are the menus. Would you like something to drink?
**Mrs. Jones:** Mineral water, please.
**Mr. Jones:** I'll have a glass of red wine.
**Mrs. Jones:** Wine at lunchtime?
**Mr. Jones:** Only one glass.

**c**
**Server:** Are you ready to order?
**Mrs. Jones:** Yes. Two steaks, please.
**Server:** How would you like the steaks?
**Mr. Jones:** Rare.
**Mrs. Jones:** Medium.

**d**
**Server:** Good afternoon, sir. Good afternoon, ma'am.
**Mr. Jones:** Good afternoon. A table for two, please.
**Server:** Sure. Smoking or non-smoking?
**Mr. Jones:** Non-smoking, please.

**e**
**Server:** Would you like to see the dessert menu?
**Mr. Jones:** Yes, please.
**Mrs. Jones:** No, thanks. You're on a diet, remember.
**Mr. Jones:** Oh, yes. I'll have an espresso, please.
**Server:** Ma'am?
**Mrs. Jones:** I'll have tea.

**2.65 Listen and check.**

**2 Look at the menu. Check (✓) the items the man and woman chose.**

### Lunch menu

**Appetizers**
- Soup of the day ☐
- Shrimp ☐
- Liver pâté ☐

**Entrées**
- Salmon ☐
- Steak ☐
- Pasta ☐

**Desserts**
- Ice cream ☐
- Apple pie ☐
- Fruit salad ☐

**Drinks**
- Red wine ☐
- White wine ☐
- Champagne ☐
- Beer ☐
- Mineral water ☐
- Cola ☐
- Hot Drinks ☐
- Espresso ☐
- Cappuccino ☐
- Tea ☐

**3 2.66 Listen and repeat the expressions.**

**a** A table for two, please.
**b** Would you like something to drink?
**c** I'll have a glass of red wine.
**d** Are you ready to order?
**e** Would you like to see the dessert menu?
**f** Could we get the check, please?

### Life Skills: Analyzing Information

Have you ever ...?

**1 Work with a partner. Complete the questionnaire.**

**Questionnaire**

**a** Have you ever *been to New York City*? Yes No
**b** Have you ever ____________? Yes No
**c** Have you ever ____________? Yes No
**d** Have you ever ____________? Yes No
**e** Have you ever ____________? Yes No
**f** Have you ever ____________? Yes No

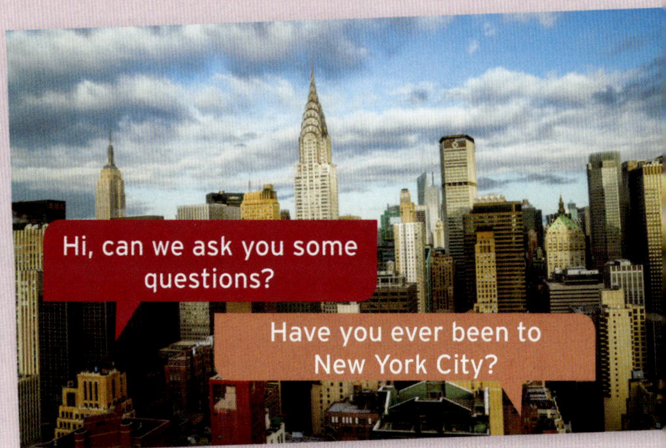


**2 Ask your questions to 5 people.**

**3 Look at the answers from your questionnaire. Create a bar chart to present the information. Write a description of your results.**

*From our questionnaire, only three people have been to New York City ...*

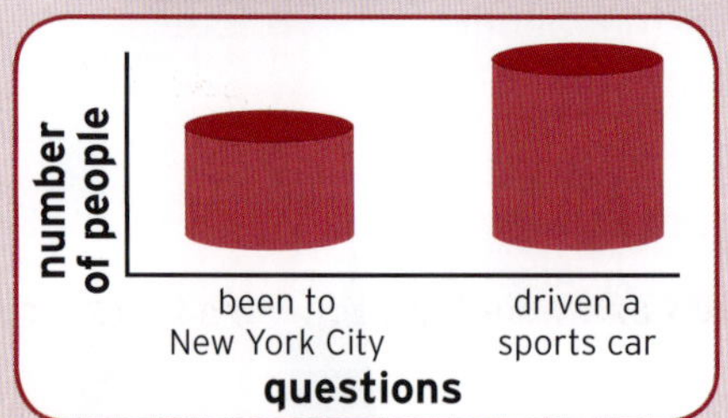


MACMILLAN LIFE SKILLS

# 11 Vocabulary Extra

## Food

**1 Match the pictures with the food.**

| | | |
|---|---|---|
| __9__ apple pie | ____ ice cream | ____ shrimp |
| ____ chicken salad | ____ melon | ____ steak and fries |
| ____ fruit salad | ____ salmon | ____ tomato soup |

**Appetizers**

**Entrées**

**Desserts**

## Drink

**2 Match the pictures with the drink.**

| | | |
|---|---|---|
| ____ red wine | ____ beer | ____ mineral water |
| ____ white wine | ____ espresso | ____ tea |

**3 Work with a partner. Cover the words. Look at the pictures. Ask and answer questions.**

What's number 9?

Apple pie. What's number 12?

## Focus on verbs + prepositions

**1 Complete the table with the verbs in the box.**

arrive ~~know~~ listen look talk wait

| Some common verbs + prepositions | Examples |
|---|---|
| **a** verb + *about* | What do you (1) __know__ **about** her? |
| | What did you (2) ____ **about**? |
| **b** verb + *at* | Don't point **at** them! |
| | They're going to (3) ____ **at** the airport at 3:00 p.m. |
| | Do you want to (4) ____ **at** pictures of my family? |
| **c** verb + *for* | How would you like to pay **for** this? |
| | Can you (5) ____ **for** me? |
| **d** verb + *to* | I explained the situation **to** him. |
| | What sort of music do you (6) ____ **to**? |

**2 Write your own example for each verb in Exercise 1.**

# 12 Drive

## READING & LISTENING

**1** 2.67 **Read the article. Add the headings: *An Italian Drive and To the Lighthouse.***

greatdrives.com

# The Greatest Drives in the World

**a** ______________________

**Where it is:** Big Sur, USA

**What it is:** The Pacific Coast Highway from Monterey to Morro Bay is one of America's greatest and most scenic drives. You can do it in a day or stay in a motel. There are great views of the ocean.

**Best car:** A Mustang

**What's the route:** Start at Monterey and drive along the ocean. The Pacific is on your right, until you reach Carmel. Drive through this small town until you get to Big Sur. You can see huge trees on your left. The road goes up 1,000 feet, and then it goes down to the beautiful beaches. Finally, drive across Bixby Creek Bridge and you can see the Point Sur Lighthouse.

**b** ______________________

**Where it is:** Stelvio Pass, Italy

**What it is:** This is a difficult drive through the Italian Alps. It's a mountain road with 60 turns. The Stelvio Pass is only 15 miles long, but it's 9,045 feet high!

**Best car:** A Ferrari

**What's the route:** This drive has great views. The best route is to drive into and then out of Stelvio National Park – then you can drive up the Stelvio Pass. At the top of the mountain, you can see very far and the scenery is amazing! As you drive down the mountain, you drive past rocks and fields – but not too fast, it can be dangerous. At the end of the Stelvio Pass, you can go to the town of Bormio, or drive to Milan.

**2 Look the sentences and write S for Stelvio Pass and B for Big Sur.**

a The drive is in Italy. ___S___
b The drive is in the USA. ______
c The road is fifteen miles long. ______
d There are sixty turns on the road. ______
e You can see a lighthouse. ______
f You can visit Carmel. ______

2.68 **Listen, repeat, and check.**

**3 Write answers to these questions.**

a What drives have you taken recently?
b Do you drive to work/school? If so, how long does it take?
c What do (or don't) you like about how you get to work/school?

- **Grammar:** Questions with prepositions. Tense review.
- **Vocabulary:** Prepositions of movement. Places in a city/countryside.
- **Language for Life:** Directions

## VOCABULARY

**1 Underline the correct preposition.**

On my way to work/school

a I go **down** / **through** the stairs.
b I go **out of** / **along** my apartment.
c I go **through** / **across** the street.
d I go **into** / **along** the river.
e I go **past** / **down** some stores.
f I go **across** / **up** a hill.
g I go **through** / **along** the park.
h I go **up** / **over** a bridge.
i I go **into** / **down** my office.

2.69 **Listen, check, and repeat.**

**2 Check (✓) the sentences in Exercise 1 that are true for your journey to work/school.**

**3 Write a detailed description of a journey you often make. Use prepositions from Exercise 1.**

*On my way to work, I go out of my house and across the street. I go …*

**Compare your description with a partner.**

### Prepositions

| | |
|---|---|
| past |  |
| through |  |
| over |  |
| along |  |
| across |  |
| up |  |
| down |  |
| into | 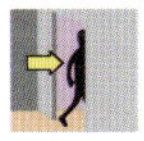 |
| out of |  |

## GRAMMAR

**1 Put the words in the correct order to make questions about a trip.**

a Where / you / from / do / start? *Where do you start from?*
b Who / with / do / travel / you?
c What / talk / about / you / do?
d What kind of music / to / do / listen / you?
e What kind of scenery / do / through / go / you?
f What kind of buildings / go / you / past / do?

2.70 **Listen, check, and repeat.**

### Questions with prepositions

Where do you come **from**?
What did you talk **about**?
What are you listening **to**?

## PRONUNCIATION

**1** 2.71 **Listen and repeat the words in the box.**

| part | through | turn | walk |
|---|---|---|---|

**2 Add the words in Exercise 1 to the list of words with the same vowel sound.**

| | | | | |
|---|---|---|---|---|
| a | /a/ | car | start | ________ |
| b | /ɜr/ | world | first | ________ |
| c | /ɔ/ | small | saw | ________ |
| d | /u/ | blue | two | ________ |

2.72 **Listen, check, and repeat.**

## LISTENING

1 2.73 **Listen to an interview about Heinz Stücke. When is he going to finish his journey?**

Heinz Stücke in 1965

2 **Answer the questions with some of the numbers in the box.**

~~10~~ 15 22 25 50 75 207 211 1960 1962

a How many times has he been around the world? 10
b When did he start his journey?
c How old was he?
d How many countries has he visited?
e How many passports has he filled?
f How many kilos does his bike weigh?

**Listen again and check.**

3 **What is the longest bicycle ride you have ever taken? Tell your partner.**

## GRAMMAR

1 **Complete the summary of Heinz Stücke's amazing journey. Underline the correct tense.**

Heinz Stücke (1) **has been / went** around the world ten times by bicycle. He (2) **has started / started** his journey forty-five years ago. He (3) **has left / left** Germany when he (4) **is / was** twenty-two years old. He (5) **has visited / visited** two hundred and eleven countries, and he (6) **has filled / filled** fifteen passports.

His bicycle (7) **weighs / has weighed** twenty-five kilos. He usually (8) **sleeps / is sleeping** in a tent and he (9) **is making / makes** money by selling postcards of his trip.

Right now, he (10) **rides / is riding** along the west coast of Nicaragua.

When (11) **does he finish / is he going to finish** his ride? He (12) **hasn't know / doesn't know**. Maybe never!

**Tense review**

Simple present: I **drive**.
Simple past: I **drove**.
Present progressive: I**'m driving**.
Future with *(be) going to*: I**'m going to drive**.
Present perfect: I've **driven**.

2.74 **Listen and check.**

2 **Pairwork Student A:** page 99 **Student B:** page 103

3 **Grammar Extra 12** page 110. Read the explanation and do the exercises.

## VOCABULARY

1 **Look at the pictures of places. Match each wordlist (a-d) with a picture (1-4).**

a trees, forest, waterfall, bridge [3]
b desert, sand, tree [ ]
c ocean, sand, rocks, beach, cliffs [ ]
d fields, grass, hills, mountains, snow [ ]

1

2

3

4

2.75 **Listen, check, and repeat.**

2 **How many things in Exercise 1 are there near your house? Put the words on a line.**

my house — x a tree — x a beach — farthest away

3 **Have you been to places like the ones in the pictures? Would you like to? Tell your partner.**

## SPEAKING: ANECDOTE

1 2.76 **Listen to Carla talking about the last time she went on an interesting road trip. Underline the correct information.**

a When did you go for a drive?
I went **last spring** / **last weekend**.
b Where did you go?
I went to **Arizona** / **North Carolina**.
c Who did you go with?
I went with **my family** / **my friend**.
d What kind of car were you in?
We were in **a Ford** / **a Corvette**.
e What time did you leave?
We left **at night** / **in the morning**.
f What was the weather like?
It was **sunny** / **raining**.
g What sort of places did you drive through?
**Hills** / **Mountains**.
h Where did you stop?
We stopped **in a small town** / **at a café**.
i What time did you get there?
We got there **in the morning** / **in the afternoon**.

2 **You are going to tell your partner about the last time you went on a road trip.**

- Ask yourself the questions in Exercise 1.
- Think *about* what to say and *how* to say it.
- Tell your partner about your drive.

Last ... I went to ...

## LANGUAGE FOR LIFE

**1 Match the pictures (1-8) with the expressions (a-h).**

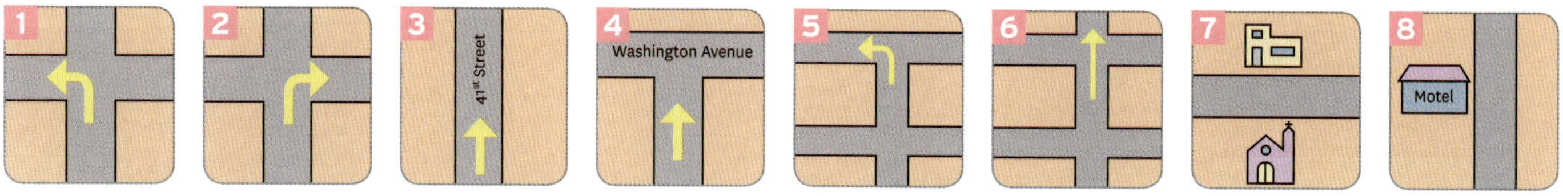


- **a** Go down Forty-First Street. 3
- **b** Across from the church. ____
- **c** Take the second street on the left. ____
- **d** Go straight. ____
- **e** There's a motel on the left. ____
- **f** Go to the end of the road, that's Washington Avenue. ____
- **g** Turn right. ____
- **h** Turn left. ____

2.77 **Listen, check, and repeat.**

**2** 2.78 **Listen to the three telephone conversations (a-c) and look at the map. Write the number (1-3) of the destination in each case.**

**3 Complete the conversation with directions from the station to destination 4.**

**A:** Hi, I'm at the station.
**B:** OK. (1) Turn right onto Lincoln Avenue. (2) ____________ the second street on the left. That's Thirty-Sixth Street.
**A:** OK.
**B:** Go (3) ____________ Thirty-Sixth Street and take the first (4) ____________ on the left.
**A:** OK.
**B:** There's a movie theater (5) ____________ the left and our house is (6) ____________ the street.
**A:** Great. See you soon.

2.79 **Listen and check.**

**4 Work with a partner. Write a similar conversation, with directions from the school to a place that you know.**

**Practice the conversation.**

### Life Skills: Problem Solving
Directions

**1** 2.80 **Listen to the directions. Is the person going to the red or green pin?**

**2 Write directions for the other color pin.**

From here, take …

**3 Draw a map of your journey from home/work to school. Explain the route you take to your partner.**

MACMILLAN LIFE SKILLS

# 12 Vocabulary Extra

## Nature

**1 Match the pictures with the nature words.**

| | | | |
|---|---|---|---|
| 5 a beach | ___ a field | ___ hills | ___ sand |
| ___ a cliff | ___ a forest | ___ a mountain | ___ a tree |
| ___ a desert | ___ grass | ___ a rock | ___ a waterfall |

**2 Work with a partner. Cover the words and look at the pictures. Ask and answer questions.**

What's number 8?

A mountain. What's number 4?

## Focus on prepositions of movement

**1 Match the pictures with the prepositional phrases.**

| | | | |
|---|---|---|---|
| 3 **across** the street | ___ **down** the stairs | ___ **out** of the house | ___ **through** the park |
| ___ **along** the river | ___ **into** the building | ___ **past** the stores | ___ **up** the hill |

**2 Work with a partner. Write another phrase for each proposition.**

across the bridge

# Review D

## GRAMMAR

Grammar Extra pages 110 and 111.

**1 Complete the text with the words in the box.**

~~going to~~ hope like to want to wouldn't like to

Next year, I'm (1) _going to_ travel to Mexico. When I'm there, I (2) ________ to do some scuba diving. But I don't (3) ________ spend all my time in the ocean. I'd (4) ________ visit Chichen Itza. I love Mexico, but I (5) ________ live there – it's too hot!

**Work with a partner. Tell each other your plans for your next vacation.**

**2 Write the questions in the correct order.**

a have / ever / you / Mexico / been / to ? _Have you ever been to Mexico?_
b ever / have / you / been / a / to / concert / rock ?
c driven / a / car / sports / your friend / has / ever ?
d visited / Australia / you / ever / have ?
e you / bought / house / a / have / ever ?
f mountain / a / ever / you / have / climbed ?

**Work with a partner. Ask and answer the questions.**

**3 Complete the conversation.**

**Tim:** (1) _Have you ever_ been to a rock concert?
**Jane:** Yes, I (2) ________.
**Tim:** When (3) ________ you go?
**Jane:** I (4) ________ last July.
**Tim:** (5) ________ you ever been to the USA?
**Jane:** No, I (6) ________.

**4 Work with a partner. Ask and answer questions about these places.**

a London
b a music festival
c a theme park
d a sports tournament
e Brazil
f the opera

**5 Complete the verbs in the correct tense.**

Hi Dad,
I'm (**1** sit) _sitting_ in a small café in Tokyo.
I (**2** eat) ________ noodle soup. Delicious! The weather (**3** be) ________ really good, and the people (**4** be) ________ friendly and helpful.
I (**5** arrive) ________ here yesterday morning.
Before that I (**6** be) ________ in Vietnam. This evening I (**7** see) ________ Yuko, a very good friend. She (**8** live) ________ here in Tokyo. She (**9** work) ________ for Sony.
I (**10** visit) ________ a lot of places in my life, but this is the first time I (**11** go) ________ to Asia. I (**12** love) ________ it!
Lots of love,
Andy

**6 Find the mistake! Cross out the incorrect sentence.**

1 a ~~I've never be to London.~~
  b I've never been to London.

2 a I wouldn't like live there.
  b I wouldn't like to live there.

3 a Have he ever been to Havana?
  b Has he ever been to Havana?

4 a She's going to meet us later.
  b She's going meet us later.

5 a I hope to go there next year.
  b I hoping to go there next year.

6 a What are you to listening?
  b What are you listening to?

## VOCABULARY

**1 Match each description with the name of a type of TV show in the box.**

documentary ~~game show~~ news reality TV show soap opera talk show

a People play games and win money. *game show*
b You find out what's happened recently in the world.
c Famous people talk about themselves and others.
d You can learn facts about people, history, or nature.
e This is a daily drama about the lives of a group of characters.
f Ordinary people, not actors, are the stars of this type of show.

**Work with a partner. Discuss your favorite type of TV show.**

**2 Write the past participles of the verbs in the box.**

buy eat go meet read swim

*buy – bought*

**3 Complete the questions with past participles from Exercise 2.**

a What's the most expensive thing you've ever *bought*?
b Have you ever ________ in a fast food restaurant?
c What's the best book you've ever ________?
d Have you ever ________ to Europe?
e Who's the most interesting person you've ever ______?
f Have you ever ________ in a lake?

**Work with a partner. Ask and answer questions.**

**4 Underline the correct preposition.**

I needed some air. I ran (1) **across / down** the stairs and (2) **out of / up** the building. I didn't know what I was doing. I went (3) **across / past** the street and started walking.
I didn't stop until I came to the river. I walked (4) **along / through** the river for a while. I went (5) **into / past** some people, but I didn't speak to them. I came to a bridge and went (6) **out of / over** it to the other side of the river.
There was a park. I walked (7) **down / through** the park and, slowly, started to feel better. I went home. I walked (8) **out of / up** the stairs and went (9) **along / into** my apartment. I sat down and fell asleep. When I woke up, I didn't know if it was all a dream, or not.

**5 Complete the nature words with *a, e, i, o, u*.**

a b*e**a*ch
b cl*i*ff
c d__s__rt
d f__ __ld
e f__r__st
f gr__ss
g h__ll
h m__ __ntain
i r__ck
j s__nd
k sn__w
l w__t__rf__ll

## PRONUNCIATION

**1 Look at some words from Units 10-12. Say the words and add them to the table.**

~~across~~ ~~adventure~~ channel ~~desert~~ dessert mountain ~~waterfall~~ along chicken tomato cartoon comedy

| | |
|---|---|
| A: ■ ▪ | *desert* |
| B: ■ ▪ ▪ | *waterfall* |
| C: ▪ ■ | *across* |
| D: ▪ ■ ▪ | *adventure* |

**2 Underline the stressed syllable in each word.**

2.81 **Listen, check, and repeat**

## READING & LISTENING

1 2.82 **Read about Malala Yousafzai. What is the name of the organization she started?**

amazingwomen.com

# Her Name is Malala

In 2014, Malala Yousafzai won the Nobel Peace Prize for her work in children's education. She was only 17 and was the youngest Nobel Prize winner ever. Malala is still very young, but a lot has happened in her life.

Malala was born in Mingora, Pakistan. Her family ran schools in the region and Malala learned that education was important for everybody. When Malala was just 11 years old she wrote a blog about her life and how difficult it was for girls to go to school. The year after, an American journalist made a short documentary about her life. She started to become more famous, and she was a finalist for the International Children's Peace Prize.

On October 9, 2012, a gunman shot Malala and she almost died. She was in hospital for a long time in Pakistan and then the UK. The attack got a lot of attention, and Malala received huge support from people around the world.

Malala has become a big supporter of education rights. She founded the Malala Fund, a charity, to help young girls with their education. She has also written a book, *I am Malala*, which has sold millions of copies around the world. Another documentary film, called *He Named Me Malala*, won many awards.

In 2017, Malala started studying at Oxford University. She is an inspiration to young women everywhere. And she's only just getting started ...

2 **Read the article again. Are the sentences true or false? Correct the false sentences.**

a Malala won the Nobel Peace Prize. True
b Malala was born in the UK.
c Malala wrote a blog when she was 17.
d Malala was shot.
e Malala has become a supporter of education rights.
f Malala has written a book, *He Named Me Malala*.

3 2.83 **Listen to the podcast. Underline the correct information.**

a Malala inspired Shawna to help **herself / children.**
b Shawna's **husband / father**, John, helped her start Blind Hope.
c Blind Hope is going to use some of the money to open a **school / hospital** in Kenya.
d Shawna is looking for **ten / twelve** people to help her.
e The trip to Kenya is going to be **a serious job / a vacation**.
f Blind Hope wants to build one school each **month / year**.

## WRITING & SPEAKING

**1 Read the email. Find the mistakes and correct them.**

Check for:
- grammar mistakes
- spelling mistakes
- missing words

Inbox
Drafts
Sent
Trash
All Mail

Drafts

Search

**Luigi Salvoni** <luigibaker@bmail.com> 9:18 a.m. (6 hours ago)
to <shawna@bmail.com>

Dear Shawna,

1
Do you remeber me? I was in your class at Willsby High School. I heared the radio show about you and Blind Hope. I'd really like to help you organization.

2
What I do after high school? Well, I became a firefighter. Then I got married Linda Danco. Do you remember her? She was in Mr. Davis's class. We moved to Kansas and had two child, a boy and a girl. Anyway, we got divorced four years ago and I move back to Cedar Rapids.

3
Now, I'm doing something diferent. I'm not a firefighter, I'm a baker! I start my own business making bread and cakes. Yes, I know I was a terrible cook at school, but I can to cook now!

4
I've also traveled a lot. I love it! I been to fifteen countries and I've done a lot of work with children.

5
I would really like to go to Kenya with Blind Hope. You think I could help? I've done some construction work before. I very strong, I love children, and I make great cakes!

Best wishes,
Luigi Salvoni

**2 Match the headings with the paragraphs (1-5) in the email.**

a His life now *Paragraph 3*
b What he did after high school
c What he would like to do next
d Introduction and the reason he's writing
e His travel and other experiences

**3 Tell your partner about yourself.**

Say ...
- what you did after elementary school / high school / college
- what interesting experiences you have had (travel, jobs)
- what your life is like now
- what you would like to do next

**4 Write an email to an old friend about what you did after elementary school / high school / college, your experiences, your life now, and what you would like to do next.**

**Exchange emails with a partner.**

Check your partner's work for:
- grammar mistakes
- spelling mistakes
- missing words

# Pairwork: Student A

## UNIT 1

**Ask Student B for the missing flight numbers and complete the table.**

What number is the flight from Milan?

| Scheduled time | Airline | Flight number | From | Status |
|---|---|---|---|---|
| 08:50 | British Airways | (1) _____ | MILAN | LANDED 08:59 |
| 09:00 | American Airlines | AA132 | NEW YORK | EXPECTED 12:23 |
| 09:35 | Alitalia | (2) _____ | ROME | LANDED 09:12 |
| 09:45 | Aeroflot | SU243 | MOSCOW | LANDED 09:22 |
| 10:00 | Iberia | (3) _____ | SEVILLE | LANDED 10:10 |
| 10:20 | Air France | AF1370 | PARIS | DELAYED |

## UNIT 2

**Ask Student B and write the names.**

What is Sam doing?

Jackie Sam Lisa

**a** __________

**b** Tom

**c** __________

**d** Shaun

**e** __________

**f** Peter

## UNIT 3

**What do you know about Student B's likes and dislikes?**
**Complete the sentences (a-f) with phrases from the box.**
**Write questions to check your sentences.**
**Ask Student B the questions to find out if you are right or wrong.**

loves likes doesn't like hates

| I think _____ (*name*) ... | Questions | ✓ = I'm right! | ✖ = I'm wrong! |
|---|---|---|---|
| a _likes_ going to clubs. | Do you like going to clubs? | ✓ | |
| b _____ swimming in the ocean. | __________ | | |
| c _____ eating in restaurants. | __________ | | |
| d _____ wearing sunglasses. | __________ | | |
| e _____ listening to classical music. | __________ | | |
| f _____ shopping for food. | __________ | | |

## UNIT 4

**Complete the *Me* column with an adverb to make the sentences true for your day time.**
**Ask Student B questions and write their answers in the *Student B* column.**
**Compare your answers. Are you similar or different?**

Do you ever read in bed?

Yes, sometimes.

| **Night time** | | |
|---|---|---|
| **Me** | **Student B** | **Similar? Different?** |
| a I _never_ read in bed. | She sometimes reads in bed. | Different |
| b I ______ sleep with my windows open. | | |
| c I ______ remember my dreams. | | |
| d I ______ sleep more than seven hours. | | |
| e I ______ wear pajamas in bed. | | |
| f I ______ sleep with the light on. | | |
| g I ______ (*your ideas*) | | |

**adverbs:** always usually often sometimes hardly ever never

## UNIT 5

**Compare the first time you did these activities with the first time Student B did them. Complete the questions with the past forms of the verbs.**
**Write your answers in the *Me* column.**
**Ask Student B the questions and write the answers in the *Student B* column.**
**Compare your answers. Are you similar or different?**

| **Questions** | **Me** | **Student B** | **Similar? Different?** |
|---|---|---|---|
| When was the first time you ... | | | |
| a (go) _went_ to a wedding? | A month ago. | | |
| b (travel) ______ alone? | | | |
| c (use) ______ a credit card? | | | |
| d (speak) ______ to a foreigner? | | | |
| e (drive) ______ a car? | | | |
| f (earn) ______ money | | | |

## UNIT 6

**What do you know about Student B?**
**Complete the sentences about Student B with a positive or negative past form of the verb.**
**Ask Student B the questions to check your sentences. Are you right or wrong?**
**Write Student B's name in the space below.**

| **I think ______ (*name*) ...** | **Questions** | **✓ = I'm right!**<br>**✗ = I'm wrong!** |
|---|---|---|
| a (like) didn't like sports at school. | Did you like sports at school? | ✗ |
| b (travel) ______ to a different country last summer. | | |
| c (pass) ______ his/her driver's test a few years ago. | | |
| d (go) ______ swimming yesterday. | | |
| e (get up) ______ early this morning. | | |
| f (buy) ______ new shoes last weekend. | | |

## UNIT 7

**Find out if you do similar things to Student B on a normal day.**
**Complete the questions with *much* or *many*.**
**Write your own answers to the questions in the *Me* column (*A lot*, *Not much/many*, *None*).**
**Ask Student B the questions and write the answers in the *Student B* column.**
**Compare your answers. Are you similar or different?**

| Questions | Me | Student B | Similar? Different? |
|---|---|---|---|
| In a normal day ... | | | |
| **a** how many emails do you send? | A lot. | Not many. | Different. |
| **b** how much water do you drink? | ______ | ______ | ______ |
| **c** how _____ CDs do you listen to? | ______ | ______ | ______ |
| **d** how _____ stores do you go in? | ______ | ______ | ______ |
| **e** how _____ money do you have on you? | ______ | ______ | ______ |
| **f** how _____ chocolate do you eat? | ______ | ______ | ______ |

## UNIT 8

**Do you have the same opinions as Student B about the town/city where you are studying?**
**Complete the questions.**
**Write your answers in the *Me* column.**
**Ask Student B the questions and write their answers in the *Student B* column.**
**Compare your answers. Are you similar or different?**

| Questions | Me | Student B | Similar? Different? |
|---|---|---|---|
| Which is ... | | | |
| **a** (ugly) the ugliest building? | _____ | _____ | Different. |
| **b** (famous) _________ park? | _____ | _____ | ______ |
| **c** (old) _________ monument? | _____ | _____ | ______ |
| **d** (expensive) _________ street? | _____ | _____ | ______ |
| **e** (big) _________ grocery store? | _____ | _____ | ______ |
| **f** (popular) _________ bar? | _____ | _____ | ______ |

## UNIT 9

**Compare how often you and Student B do the following things.**
**Write your answers in the *Me* column.**
**Ask Student B the questions and write their answers in the *Student B* column.**
**Compare your answers. Are you similar or different?**

| Questions | Me | Student B | Similar? Different? |
|---|---|---|---|
| **a** How often do you go on vacation? | _____ | _____ | Different. |
| **b** How often do you go to the dentist? | _____ | _____ | ______ |
| **c** How often do you exercise? | _____ | _____ | ______ |
| **d** How often do you check your emails? | _____ | _____ | ______ |
| **e** How often do you buy a lottery ticket? | _____ | _____ | ______ |
| **f** How often do you _____ (*your ideas*)? | _____ | _____ | ______ |

## UNIT 10

**Do you have similar future plans and intentions to Student B?**
**Write your answers in the *Me* column with a ✓, ✖ or ?**
**Ask Student B the questions and write their answers in the *Student B* column.**
**Compare your answers. Who plans the most?**

**KEY**

✓ = Yes, I am.
✖ = No, I'm not.
? = I don't know.

| Questions | Me | Student B |
|---|---|---|
| a Are you going to walk home after class? | ____ | ____ |
| b Are you going to send any emails this evening? | ____ | ____ |
| c Are you going to have lunch at home tomorrow? | ____ | ____ |
| d Are you going out on Saturday night? | ____ | ____ |
| e Are you going to study in the next few days? | ____ | ____ |
| f Are you going to go somewhere interesting next week? | ____ | ____ |

## UNIT 11

**What experiences has Student B had?**
**Write Student B's name in the space below. Read the experiences.**
**Underline *has* or *hasn't* based on what you think.**
**Ask Student B questions to check if you are right or wrong.**

| I think ______ (*name*) ... | Questions | ✓= I'm right!<br>✖ = I'm wrong! |
|---|---|---|
| a **has** / **hasn't** been to New York | Have you been to New York? | ✖ |
| b **has** / **hasn't** worked in a store | ______________ | |
| c **has** / **hasn't** bought a movie online | ______________ | |
| d **has** / **hasn't** met someone/anyone with the same name | ______________ | |
| e **has** / **hasn't** swum in a river | ______________ | |
| f **has** / **hasn't** driven a Mercedes | ______________ | |

## UNIT 12

**Compare yourself with Student B.**
**Underline the correct verb form for each question.**
**Write your answers to the questions in the *Me* column.**
**Ask Student B the questions and write their answers in the *Student B* column.**
**Compare your answers. Are you similar or different?**

| Questions | Me | Student B | Similar? Different? |
|---|---|---|---|
| a How often **do you go** / **are you going** swimming? | ____ | ____ | ________ |
| b What time **did you get up** / **have you got up** yesterday? | ____ | ____ | ________ |
| c What book **do you read** / **are you reading** right now? | ____ | ____ | ________ |
| d What **are you going to do** / **do you do** this evening? | ____ | ____ | ________ |
| e How many times **are you go** / **have you been** to the USA? | ____ | ____ | ________ |
| f What kind of music **are you liking** / **do you like**? | ____ | ____ | ________ |

# Pairwork: Student B

## UNIT 1

**Ask Student A for the missing flight numbers and complete the table.**

What number is the flight from New York?

| Scheduled time | Airline | Flight number | From | Status |
|---|---|---|---|---|
| 08:50 | British Airways | BA561 | MILAN | LANDED 08:59 |
| 09:00 | American Airlines | (1) _____ | NEW YORK | EXPECTED 12:23 |
| 09:35 | Alitalia | AZ200 | ROME | LANDED 09:12 |
| 09:45 | Aeroflot | (2) _____ | MOSCOW | LANDED 09:22 |
| 10:00 | Iberia | IB4144 | SEVILLE | LANDED 10:10 |
| 10:20 | Air France | (3) _____ | PARIS | DELAYED |

## UNIT 2

**Ask Student A and write the names.**

Peter Tom Shaun

What is Peter doing?

a Sam

b __________

c Jackie

d __________

e Lisa

f __________

## UNIT 3

**What do you know about Student A's likes and dislikes?**
**Complete the sentences (a-f) with phrases from the box.**
**Write questions to check your sentences.**
**Ask Student A the questions to find out if you are right or wrong.**

loves likes doesn't like hates

| I think _____ (*name*) ... | Questions | ✓ = I'm right! | ✖ = I'm wrong! |
|---|---|---|---|
| a likes going to parties. | Do you like going to parties? | ✓ | |
| b _______ running. | ____________________ | | |
| c _______ eating hamburgers. | ____________________ | | |
| d _______ wearing jeans. | ____________________ | | |
| e _______ listening to jazz. | ____________________ | | |
| f _______ shopping for clothes. | ____________________ | | |

## UNIT 4

**Complete the *Me* column with an adverb to make the sentences true for your day time.**
**Ask Student A questions and write the answers in the *Student A* column.**
**Compare your answers. Are you similar or different?**

Do you ever read get up after 10:00 a.m.?

Yes, sometimes.

| Day time | | |
|---|---|---|
| **Me** | **Student A** | **Similar? Different?** |
| a I __never__ get up after 10:00 a.m. | He sometimes gets up after 10:00 a.m. | Different |
| b I ______ have black coffee for breakfast. | ______ | ______ |
| c I ______ walk to work/school. | ______ | ______ |
| d I ______ meet friends for lunch. | ______ | ______ |
| e I ______ make dinner for the family. | ______ | ______ |
| f I ______ go to bed before midnight. | ______ | ______ |
| g I ______ (*your ideas*) | ______ | ______ |

**adverbs:** always usually often hardly ever never

## UNIT 5

**Compare the first time you did these activities with the first time Student A did them.**
**Complete the questions with the past forms of the verbs.**
**Write your answers in the *Me* column.**
**Ask Student A the questions and write their answers in the *Student A* column.**
**Compare your answers. Are you similar or different?**

| Questions | Me | Student A | Similar? Different? |
|---|---|---|---|
| When was the last time you ... | | | |
| a (have) __had__ a haircut? | Last week. | ______ | ______ |
| b (call) ______ your mother? | ______ | ______ | ______ |
| c (make) ______ dinner for someone? | ______ | ______ | ______ |
| d (hold) ______ a baby? | ______ | ______ | ______ |
| e (give) ______ someone a gift? | ______ | ______ | ______ |
| f (take) ______ a picture? | ______ | ______ | ______ |

## UNIT 6

**What do you know about Student A?**
**Complete the sentences about Student A with a positive or negative past form of the verb.**
**Ask Student A the questions to check your sentences. Are you right or wrong?**

| I think ______ (*name*) ... | Questions | ✓ = I'm right!<br>✖ = I'm wrong! |
|---|---|---|
| a (go) __went__ skiing last winter. | Did you go skiing last winter? | ✓ |
| b (play) ______ a musical instrument at school. | ______ | |
| c (drive) ______ to work/school this morning. | ______ | |
| d (watch) ______ a good movie last night. | ______ | |
| e (have) ______ lunch alone yesterday. | ______ | |
| f (visit) ______ relatives last weekend. | ______ | |

## UNIT 7

**Find out if you do similar things to Student A on a normal day.**
**Complete the questions with *much* or *many*.**
**Write your own answers to the questions in the *Me* column (*A lot, Not much/many, None*).**
**Ask Student A the questions and write the answers in the *Student A* column.**
**Compare your answers. Are you similar or different?**

| Questions | Me | Student A | Similar? Different? |
|---|---|---|---|
| In a normal day ... | | | |
| a how much coffee do you drink? | Not much. | None. | Different. |
| b how many cookies do you eat? | ______ | ______ | ______ |
| c how _____ shows do you watch on TV? | ______ | ______ | ______ |
| d how _____ time do you spend online? | ______ | ______ | ______ |
| e how _____ phone calls do you make? | ______ | ______ | ______ |
| f how _____ keys do you have on you? | ______ | ______ | ______ |

## UNIT 8

**Do you have the same opinions as Student A about the town/city where you are studying?**
**Complete the questions.**
**Write your answers in the *Me* column.**
**Ask Student A the questions and write their answers in the *Student A* column.**
**Compare your answers. Are you similar or different?**

| Questions | Me | Student A | Similar? Different? |
|---|---|---|---|
| Which is ... | | | |
| a (interesting) the most interesting building? | _____ | _____ | Similar. |
| b (beautiful) ______________ park? | _____ | _____ | ______ |
| c (modern) ______________ monument? | _____ | _____ | ______ |
| d (busy) ______________ street? | _____ | _____ | ______ |
| e (cheap) ______________ grocery store? | _____ | _____ | ______ |
| f (quiet) ______________ bar? | _____ | _____ | ______ |

## UNIT 9

**Compare how often you and Student A do the following things.**
**Write your answers in the *Me* column.**
**Ask Student A the questions and write their answers in the *Student A* column.**
**Compare your answers. Are you similar or different?**

| Questions | Me | Student A | Similar? Different? |
|---|---|---|---|
| a How often do you go clubbing? | _____ | _____ | Similar. |
| b How often do you go to the hairdresser? | _____ | _____ | ______ |
| c How often do you do the housework? | _____ | _____ | ______ |
| d How often do you check your bank balance? | _____ | _____ | ______ |
| e How often do you buy a newspaper? | _____ | _____ | ______ |
| f How often do you _____ (*your ideas*)? | _____ | _____ | ______ |

## UNIT 10

**Do you have similar future plans and intentions to Student A?**
**Write your answers in the *Me* column with a ✓, ✖ or ?**
**Ask Student A the questions and write their answers in the *Student A* column.**
**Compare your answers. Who plans the most?**

**KEY**

✓ = Yes, I am.
✖ = No, I'm not.
? = I don't know.

| Questions | Me | Student A |
|---|---|---|
| a Are you going to drive home after class? | ____ | ____ |
| b Are you going to cook dinner this evening? | ____ | ____ |
| c Are you going to have lunch in a restaurant tomorrow? | ____ | ____ |
| d Are you going out on Friday night? | ____ | ____ |
| e Are you going to do any sports in the next few days? | ____ | ____ |
| f Are you going to do something interesting next week? | ____ | ____ |

## UNIT 11

**What experiences has Student A had?**
**Write Student A's name in the space below. Read the experiences.**
**Underline *has* or *hasn't* based on what you think.**
**Ask Student A questions to check if you are right or wrong.**

| I think ______ (*name*) ... | Questions | ✓= I'm right!<br>✖ = I'm wrong! |
|---|---|---|
| a <u>has</u> / **hasn't** been to London | Have you been to London? | ✖ |
| b **has** / **hasn't** worked in a restaurant | ____________ | |
| c **has** / **hasn't** bought a book online | ____________ | |
| d **has** / **hasn't** met someone/anyone with the same birthday | ____________ | |
| e **has** / **hasn't** swum in a lake | ____________ | |
| f **has** / **hasn't** driven a BMW | ____________ | |

## UNIT 12

**Compare yourself with Student A.**
**Underline the correct verb form for each question.**
**Write your answers to the questions in the *Me* column.**
**Ask Student A the questions and write their answers in the *Student A* column.**
**Compare your answers. Are you similar or different?**

| Questions | Me | Student A | Similar? Different? |
|---|---|---|---|
| a How often <u>**do you play**</u> / **are you playing** chess? | ____ | ____ | ________ |
| b What time **did you go** / **have you gone** to bed yesterday? | ____ | ____ | ________ |
| c What color shoes **do you wear** / **are you wearing** right now? | ____ | ____ | ________ |
| d What **are you going to have** / **do you have** for dinner this evening? | ____ | ____ | ________ |
| e How many times **are you go** / **have you been** to Canada? | ____ | ____ | ________ |
| f What kind of TV show **are you liking** / **do you like**? | ____ | ____ | ________ |

# Grammar Extra

## UNIT 1: Nouns; a/an

### Regular forms

| Singular | Plural | Spelling |
|---|---|---|
| a book | book**s** | Add *s*. |
| a toothbrush | toothbrush**es** | Add *es* after *ch, sh, s, x*. |
| a library | librar**ies** | Add *ies* after a consonant + *y*. |

### Irregular forms

| Singular | Plural |
|---|---|
| a person | people |
| a child | children |
| a man | men |
| a woman | women |

### a or an?

You use **a** before a consonant sound: ***a b****ook*, ***a k****ey*
You use **an** before a vowel sound: ***an a****pple*, ***an u****mbrella*

### there is/there are; some/any

| | Affirmative | Negative |
|---|---|---|
| **Singular** | **There's** (**is**) a beach. | **There isn't** (**is not**) a restaurant. |
| **Plural** | **There are** some people. | **There aren't** (**are not**) any people. |

With plurals, you use ***some*** in affirmative sentences if you don't want to give an exact number.
*There are **some** people.*
With plurals, you use ***any*** in negative sentences and questions.
*There aren't **any** bars. Are there **any** hotels?*

| | Question | Short answer *Yes* | Short answer *No* |
|---|---|---|---|
| **Singular** | **Is there** a doctor? | Yes, **there is.** | No, **there isn't.** |
| **Plural** | **Are there** any hotels? | Yes, **there are.** | No, **there aren't.** |

## UNIT 2: Present progressive

| Affirmative | Negative |
|---|---|
| **I'm** (**am**) **working.** | **I'm not** (**am not**) **working.** |
| You/We/They**'re** (**are**) **working.** | You/We/They **aren't** (**are not**) **working.** |
| He/She/It**'s** (**is**) **working.** | He/She/It **isn't working.** |

You use the present progressive to talk about activities in progress now.

**Spelling *ing* forms**
Delete **e** and add ***ing*** for verbs that end in **e**:
have - hav**ing**, make - mak**ing**
Add consonant + *ing* for verbs that end in a stressed vowel + a consonant: run - runn**ing**, stop - stopp**ing**

| Question | Short answer *Yes* | Short answer *No* |
|---|---|---|
| **Am** I **working**? | Yes, I **am**. | No, I**'m not**. |
| **Are** you/we/they **working**? | Yes, you/we/they **are**. | No, you/we/they **aren't**. |
| **Is** he/she/it **working**? | Yes, he/she/it **is**. | No, he/she/it **isn't**. |

### Possession

| **A subject pronoun** | I | you | he | she | it | we | they |
|---|---|---|---|---|---|---|---|
| **Possessive determiner** | my | your | his | her | its | our | their |

You use the same possessive determiner for singular and plural:
**our** *family* / **our** *friends* (NOT ~~ours friends~~)
You use *his* for a man and *her* for a woman:
*Bill and **his** wife = Bill's wife*
*Hillary and **her** husband = Hillary's husband*

**Possessive *'s* or *s'*?**
You use *'s* for one person:
***my brother's school / my brother's friends***
( = I have one brother)
You use *s'* for more than one person:
***my brothers' school / my brothers' friends***
(= I have two or more brothers)

## UNIT 1: Exercises

1 Underline the correct form.
Near my home ...

a there are **any** / **some** stores.
b there's **a** / **any** hotel.
c there are **some** / **a** bars.
d there's **an** / **some** Italian restaurant.
e there's **any** / **a** park.
f there are **some** / **a** trees.

2 Write the sentences in Exercise 1 in the negative.

a *... there aren't any stores.*

3 Check (✓) the sentences in Exercise 1 and 2 that are true for you.

## UNIT 2: Exercises

1 Complete the table with the verbs in the box.

~~come~~ ~~eat~~ ~~get~~ have listen to make hope read run sit sleep study talk use wear write

| verbs ending in *e* | verbs ending in one vowel + one consonant | all other verbs |
|---|---|---|
| *come – coming* | *get – getting* | *eat – eating* |

2 Complete the email.

Inbox
Drafts
Sent
Trash
All Mail

Drafts

Search

Dear Aunt Ellen,
We (1 have) *'re having* a great time in Costa Rica. I (2 sit) ______________ on the beach and I (3 drink) ______________ a delicious fruit juice. Joe (4 read) ______________ a book and he (5 listen) ______________ to music on his phone. Madison (6 swim) ______________ in the ocean and Perry (7 sleep) ______________ in the hotel. He went dancing last night. We (8 eat) ______________ a lot of good food, and I (9 get) ______________ fat!
We (10 think) ______________ of you,
Love Debra, Joe, Madison, and Perry
xxx

## UNIT 3: Simple present

| Affirmative | Negative |
|---|---|
| I/You/We/They **work**. | I/You/We/They **don't** (**do not**) **work**. |
| He/She/It **works**. | He/She/It **doesn't** (**does not**) **work**. |

| Question | Short answer *Yes* | Short answer *No* |
|---|---|---|
| **Do** I/you/we/they **work**? | Yes, I/you/we/they **do**. | No, I/you/we/they **don't**. |
| **Does** he/she/it **work**? | Yes, he/she/it **does**. | No, he/she/it **doesn't**. |

In questions, you put *do*/*does* before the subject.
***Do** you work in a school?*
(NOT ~~*You work in a school?*~~)

**Spelling he/she/it verb endings**
Add *s* after most verbs: live - live**s**, work - work**s**
Add *es* after *ch*, *sh*, *s*, *x*: watch - watch**es**, finish - finish**es**
Delete *y* and add *ies* for verbs that end in a consonant + *y*: study - stud**ies**
Irregular forms: do - **does**, go - **goes**, have - **has**

## UNIT 4: Adverbs of frequency

| 100% | | | | | 0% |
|---|---|---|---|---|---|
| **always** | **usually** | **often** | **sometimes** | **hardly ever** | **never** |

You use adverbs of frequency before a main verb.
*I **always** have coffee for breakfast. (NOT ~~I have always coffee ...~~)*
*He doesn't **usually** drink beer. (NOT ~~He doesn't drink usually beer.~~)*
You use adverbs of frequency after *be (am/are/is)*.
She's **always** happy. (NOT - ~~*She always is happy*~~.)

### Time

It's twelve o'clock.
It's five to.
It's five after.
It's ten to.
It's ten after.
It's a quarter to.
It's a quarter after.
It's twenty to.
It's twenty after.
It's twenty-five to.
It's twenty-five after.
It's twelve thirty.

You can ask:
*What time is it?*
You can use *It's* + time to answer the question.
It's *six o'clock*.

## UNIT 5: Simple past: affirmative

| Affirmative |
|---|
| I/You/He/She/it/We/They **worked, played, went, had,** etc. |

There is only one past form for every verb (except *be* = *was/were*).
**Spelling regular verbs**
Add *ed* or *d* after most verbs: work - work**ed**, demonstrate - demonstrat**ed**
Delete *y* and add *ied* for verbs that end in a consonant + *y*: study - stud**ied**, try - tr**ied**
Add consonant + *ed* for verbs that end in a stressed vowel + a consonant: stop - stopp**ed**, plan - plann**ed**

## UNIT 3: Exercises

**1 Complete the sentences with *I* or *My teacher*.**

a ___I___ live in a city.
b ______ like doing housework.
c ______ wears a watch.
d ______ work in a store.
e ______ speaks French.
f ______ has a cell phone.
g ______ study computer science.
h ______ does yoga.

**Write the sentences in the negative.**
**Check (✓) the true sentences.**

**2 Write the questions in the correct order.**

a Do / the guitar / play / you ? Do you play the guitar?
b your friends / study / Do / English ?
c smoke / Does / your teacher ?
d drive / a big car / your father / Does ?
e you / coffee / Do / drink ?
f to the gym / Does / go / your mother ?

**Answer the questions.**

a Yes, I do.

## UNIT 4: Exercises

**1 Put the words in the correct order.**

a Tom / happy / always / is .
Tom is always happy.
b Janet / sometimes / for breakfast / has eggs .
c Dirk / on Saturday evenings / goes out / usually .
d Sue / tired / on Friday evenings / often / is .
e Harry / does the housework / hardly ever .
f Maggie / answers / her cell phone / never .

**2 Replace the names in Exercise 1 with people you know.**
**Make true sentences.**

a My grandfather is always happy.

**3 Add adverbs of frequency to make true sentences.**

a I speak English in class.
I always speak English in class.
b I'm late for my English class.
c I get emails in English.
d I speak English at work.
e I use English on vacation.
f I read magazines and books in English.

## UNIT 5: Exercises

**1 Complete the table for these regular verbs.**

| verb | simple past form |
|---|---|
| a work | worked |
| b call | ______ |
| c ______ | stopped |
| d study | ______ |
| e like | ______ |
| f complete | ______ |
| g ______ | tried |
| h ______ | listened |

**2 Complete the sentences with these irregular verbs.**

a I (go) __went__ to a party last Saturday.
b I (wear) ______ jeans yesterday.
c I (see) ______ a good movie two weeks ago.
d I (be) ______ very tired last night.
e I (sit) ______ on the beach last weekend.
f I (wake up) ______ before seven o'clock this morning.

**3 Change the time expressions to make the sentences in Exercise 2 true for you.**

## UNIT 6: Simple past: affirmative, negative, and question forms

| **Affirmative** | **Negative** |
|---|---|
| I/You/He/She/it/We/They **worked**. | I/You/He/She/it/We/They **didn't** (**did not**) **work**. |

| **Question** | **Short answer *Yes*** | **Short answer *No*** |
|---|---|---|
| **Did** I/you/he/she/it/we/they **work**? | Yes, I/you/he/she/it/we/they **did**. | No, I/you/he/she/it/we/they **didn't**. |

In questions, you put *Did* before the subject.
***Did*** *you go shopping?* (NOT ~~*You went shopping?*~~)
You don't use *Did* with *be*.
*Were you at home yesterday?* (NOT *Did you be at home yesterday?*)

## UNIT 7: Countable and uncountable nouns

| **Affirmative** | | |
|---|---|---|
| **Countable nouns** | | **Uncountable nouns** |
| **Singular** | **Plural** | |
| a melon | two melons | some milk (NOT ~~one milk~~) |
| a grape | some grapes | some pasta (NOT ~~three pastas~~) |

| **Negative and question: *How many ...? / How much ...?*** | |
|---|---|
| **Countable nouns** | **Uncountable nouns** |
| **How many** apples are there? | **How much** cheese is there? |
| There are **a lot**. | There's **a lot**. |
| There are**n't many**. | There is**n't much**. |
| There are**n't any**. | There is**n't any**. |

You use *a lot (of)* in affirmative sentences.
*I eat* **a lot of** *bread.*
*I meet* **a lot of** *people*.

You use *much/many* in negative sentences and questions.
*I don't drink* ***much*** *coffee.*
*I don't read* ***many*** *books.*
*Do you drink* ***much*** *coffee?*
*Do you eat* ***many*** *cookies?*

## UNIT 8: Comparative and superlative adjectives

| | **Adjective** | **Comparative** | **Superlative** |
|---|---|---|---|
| **Short adjectives: add *er/est*** | | | |
| Adjectives ending in a consonant or **e** | old nice | old**er** nic**er** | the old**est**<br>the nic**est** |
| Adjectives ending in a vowel + a consonant | big | big**ger** | the big**gest** |
| Adjectives ending in ***y*** | happ**y** | happ**ier** | the happ**iest** |
| **Irregular adjectives** | good bad far | better worse farther | the best the worst the farthest |
| **Long adjectives: add *more / the most*** | interesting | **more** interesting | **the most** interesting |

You use comparative adjectives to compare people/things with other people/things.
*China is* ***bigger than*** *India.*
*Gold is* ***more valuable than*** *silver.*
You use superlative adjectives to compare people/things with all the other people/things in their group.
*Russia is* ***the biggest*** *country.*
*Platinum is* ***the most valuable*** *metal.*

## UNIT 6: Exercises

1 **Write sentences in the negative.**

a I got up late.
*I didn't get up late.*
b I wore jeans.
c I did the housework.
d I played tennis.
e I had lunch with my family.
f I went shopping.
g I bought a DVD.
h I read the newspaper.

2 **Think about last Sunday. Check (✓) the affirmative or negative sentences in Exercise 1 that are true for you.**

3 **Write simple past questions with *you* for the sentences in Exercise 1.**

a *Did you get up late last Sunday?*

4 **Ask your partner the questions in Exercise 3.**

## UNIT 7: Exercises

1 **Make sentences with *I*, and complete the table. Use *a lot of*, *not much*, or *not many*.**

| | Affirmative | Negative |
|---|---|---|
| a eat bread | *I eat a lot of bread.* | *I don't eat much bread.* |
| b drink coffee | | |
| c do exercise | | |
| d read books | | |
| e buy magazines | | |
| f get emails | | |
| g meet people | | |
| h have free time | | |

**Check (✓) the affirmative or negative sentences that are true for you.**

2 **Write questions with *How much ...?* or *How many ...?* about the topics in Exercise 1.**

a *How much bread do you eat?*

**Ask your partner the questions.**

## UNIT 8: Exercises

1 **Write sentences comparing the things below. Use the adjectives (in parentheses).**

a Driving / flying (dangerous)
*Driving is more dangerous than flying.*
b Mexican food / Chinese food (good)
c Meat / fish (healthy)
d English / my language (difficult)
e Men / women (romantic)
f Cats / dogs (nice)

**Compare your ideas with a partner.**

2 **Use the prompts and write sentences about people or places you know. Use superlative forms.**

a beach (beautiful)
*The most beautiful beach I know is Ipanema beach in Rio de Janeiro.*
b city (ugly)
c restaurant (expensive)
d person (funny)
e driver (bad)
f person (lucky)

**Talk about your sentences with a partner.**

## UNIT 9: can

| Affirmative | Negative |
|---|---|
| I/You/He/She/It/ We/They **can swim.** | I/You/He/She/It/ We/They **can't (cannot) swim.** |

| Question | Short answer *Yes* | Short answer *No* |
|---|---|---|
| **Can** I /you/he/she/it/ we/they **swim**? | Yes, I/you/he/she/it/we/they **can**. | No, I/you/he/she/it/we/they **can't**. |

You use *can* to talk about ability. You put *can* before the subject in questions.
***Can you*** *swim?* (NOT ~~*You can swim?*~~)
You don't use ***to*** after ***can***.
*I* ***can*** *swim.* (NOT ~~*I can to swim*~~)

## UNIT 10: (be) going to

| Affirmative | Negative |
|---|---|
| I**'m** (**am**) **going to come.** | **I'm not** (**am not**) **going to come.** |
| You/We/They**'re** (**are**) **going to come.** | You/We/They **aren't** (**are not**) **going to come.** |
| He/She/It**'s** (**is**) **going to come.** | He/She/It **isn't** (**is not**) **going to come.** |

| Question | Short answer *Yes* | Short answer *No* |
|---|---|---|
| **Am I going to come**? | Yes, I **am**. | No, I**'m not**. |
| **Are** you/we/they **going to come**? | Yes, you/we/they **are**. | No, you/we/they/**aren't**. |
| **Is** he/she/it **going to come**? | Yes, he/she/it **is**. | No, he/she/it **isn't**. |

You use ***(be) going to*** to talk about your future plans and intentions.

## UNIT 11: Present perfect

| Affirmative | Negative |
|---|---|
| I/You/We/They**'ve** (**have**) **worked**. | I/You/We/They **haven't** (**have not**) **worked**. |
| He/She/It's (**has**) **worked**. | He/She/It **hasn't** (**has not**) **worked**. |

| Question | Short answer *Yes* | Short answer *No* |
|---|---|---|
| **Have** I/you/we/they **worked?** | Yes, I/you/we/they **have**. | No, I/you/we/they **haven't** (**have not**). |
| **Has** he/she/it **worked?** | Yes, he/she/it **has**. | No, he/she/it **hasn't** (**has not**). |

You use the present perfect to talk about completed actions in "time up to now." You don't focus on when.
***ever*** = at any time in your life

## UNIT 12: Tense review

| Tense | Uses | Affirmative | Negative | Question |
|---|---|---|---|---|
| Simple present | Facts/habits/routines | He **works**. | He **doesn't work**. | **Does** he **work**? |
| Simple past | Completed action at a specific past time | She **worked** yesterday. | She **didn't work** yesterday. | **Did** she **work** yesterday? |
| Present progressive | Activities in progress now | They**'re working** now. | They **aren't working** now. | **Are** they **working** now? |
| Future with *(be) going to* | Future plans and intentions | We**'re going to work** tomorrow. | We **aren't going to work** tomorrow. | **Are** we **going to work** tomorrow? |
| Present perfect | Completed action in "time up to now" | It's **worked** recently. | It **hasn't worked** recently. | **Has** it **worked** recently? |

## UNIT 9: Exercises

1 **Write sentences with *can* and *can't.***

- a I / English / not Spanish. (speak)
  I can speak English, but I can't speak Spanish.
- b I / a bicycle / not a motorcycle. (ride)
- c I / a car / not a bus. (drive)
- d I / the guitar / not the drums. (play)
- e I / music / not Japanese. (read)
- f I / chess / not poker. (play)

2 **Rewrite the sentences in Exercise 1 with *and* or *but* to make them all true for you.**

I can speak English and I can speak Spanish.
I can ride a bicycle, but I can't ride a motorcycle.

## UNIT 10: Exercises

1 **Write true sentences about tomorrow with *I'm going to* or *I'm not going to.***

- a buy a car
  I'm not going to buy a car tomorrow.
- b get up early
- c see my parents
- d play golf
- e watch my favorite TV show
- f wear jeans

2 **Write questions with *you* and *your* for the sentences in Exercise 1. Then ask your partner.**

a Are you going to buy a new car tomorrow?

3 **Look at the picture of Jane's shopping. Write sentences about her plans for this evening.**

a She's going to have pizza.

## UNIT 11: Exercises

1 **Write the sentences in the negative.**

- a I've been to New York.
  I haven't been to New York.
- b I've seen the Pyramids in Egypt.
- c I've driven in a foreign country.
- d I've stayed in a five-star hotel.
- e I've eaten sushi.
- f I've slept on a beach.

2 **Check (✓) the affirmative or negative sentences in Exercise 1 that are true for you.**

3 **Write questions with *you* and *ever* for the sentences in Exercise 1.**

a Have you ever been to New York?

4 **Ask your partner the questions in Exercise 3. Write the answers.**

a Donna hasn't been to New York.

b She's …

## UNIT 12: Exercises

1 **Name the verb tense used in the sentences.**

- a I *listen* to American hip-hop. Simple present
- b I *saw* a movie in English last month.
- c I'*ve written* emails in English at work.
- d I'*m studying* for an English exam right now.
- e I'*m going to take* an English language course next summer.
- f I *like* speaking English.

2 **Write the sentences in Exercise 1 in the negative.**

a I don't listen to American hip-hop.

**Check (✓) the affirmative or negative sentences in Exercise 1 or 2 that are true for you.**

# Audioscript

## Unit 1

1.04

1 Portuguese
2 German
3 Italian
4 Spanish
5 English
6 Spanish
7 Chinese
8 Japanese

1.05

a Is he Chinese?
Yes, he is./No, he isn't.
b Are they Spanish?
Yes, they are./No, they aren't.
c Is it Japanese?
Yes, it is./No, it isn't.
d Is she Mexican?
Yes, she is./No, she isn't.
e Is it German?
Yes, it is./No, it isn't.
f Are they British?
Yes, they are./No, they aren't.

1.08

a A E I O U
b A I O E U
c E I A U O
d I A O U E
e I U A O E

1.10

a The number for LATAM is 1-866-435-9526.
b The number for American Airlines is 800-433-7300.
c The number for British Airways is 0344 493 0787.
d The number for Air Canada is 1-514-393-3333.
e The number for TAP is 1800 221 73 70.
f The number for United Airlines is 1-800-864-8331.

1.13

1 a magazine - magazines
2 an iPad - iPads
3 an umbrella - umbrellas
4 a pen - pens

1.14

a What's this?/It's a book.
b What are these?/They're pens.
c What are these?/They're keys.
d What are these?/They're coins.
e What's this? /It's a bag.
f What are these? /They're watches.

1.18

**(S = Student; T = Teacher)**
**S:** How do you say "Francia" in English?
**T:** "France".
**S:** How do you spell it?
**T:** F-R-A-N-C-E.
**S:** Ah, yes. "France." How do you say "Itália" in English?
**T:** "Italy."
**S:** How do you spell it?
**T:** I-T-A-L-Y.
**S:** Oh, yes. "Italy." English is easy. How do you say "Alemania"?
**T:** "Germany."
**S:** Excuse me?
**T:** "Germany."
**S:** How do you spell it?
**T:** G-E-R-M-A-N-Y.
**S:** Can you repeat that, please?
**T:** G-E-R-M-A-N-Y.
**S:** OK, thanks.

1.20

a
**Student:** Is the answer "Italy"?
**Teacher:** Yes, that's right. Well done.
**Student:** Thank you.

b
**Student:** Is the answer "Spain"?
**Teacher:** No, it's not. Please look at the question again.
**Student:** Ah, is the answer "Spanish"?

c
**Student:** I don't know how to write it.
**Teacher:** Please try.
**Student:** OK.

## Unit 2

1.21

a This is me and my brother, Zach. He's so great.
b My older sister, Louise, getting married to my new brother-in-law, Andy. What a day!
c My lovely parents. Smile, mom and dad!
d My uncle Tony and my aunt Jean with my cousins Tom, and Sally.
e My best friend, Carey, with her son and daughter. Hi, guys!
f Two of my favorite cousins, Frank and Nina!

1.22

a I'm a singer. My sister is Solange Knowles.
b He's from Springfield, in the USA. His son's name is Bart.
c She's from Britain. Her albums include *21* and *25*.
d We're married. Our names are Kanye and Kim.
e They're American. Their last name is Clinton.

1.24

a thirteen
b fourteen
c fifty
d sixteen
e seventy

1.26

a She's nineteen.
b He's sixty-four.
c She's forty-one.
d He's nine.

1.28

a 23% of dentists are women.
b 28% of doctors are women.
c 91% of nurses are women.
d 13% of police officers are women.
e 35% of lawyers are women.
f 93% of hairdressers are women.
g 51% of sales clerks are women.
h 6% of taxi drivers are women.

1.30

**Singular nouns:**
an overcoat, a jacket, a shirt, a suit, a skirt, a tie, a dress, a sweater, a top, a T-shirt, a belt, a hat, a ring
**Plural nouns:**
a pair of boots, a pair of shoes, a pair of sneakers, a pair of pants, a pair of jeans, a pair of sweatpants, a pair of sunglasses

1.32

**(I = Interviewer; C = Customer)**

a
**I:** Hi, I see you're looking at The Clothing Company website.
Can I ask you a couple of questions about it?
**C:** Sure.
**I:** What are you looking for?
**C:** I'm looking for a new skirt.
**I:** Are you looking for something formal or casual?
**C:** Formal. I'm a lawyer and need to look smart.
**I:** Can I ask how much you are looking to spend?
**C:** About 50 dollars.
**I:** Great, thanks.

b
**I:** Hi, there. I see you're looking at The Clothing Company website.
Can I ask you a couple of questions?
**C:** No problem
**I:** What are you looking for today?
**C:** I'm looking for a pair of boots.
**I:** What are they for?
**C:** For work. I'm a sales clerk and have to stand all day!
**I:** Can I ask how much you are looking to spend?
**C:** About 30 dollars.
**I:** Great, thanks.

c
**I:** Hi, I see you're looking at The Clothing Company website. May I ask you some questions about it?
**C:** Go ahead.
**I:** Can I ask what are you looking for?
**C:** I'm looking for a pair of sunglasses.
**I:** Are these for work?
**C:** That's right. As a police officer I'm outside in the sun most of the day.
**I:** And how much you are looking to spend?
**C:** Only 10 dollars if *they* have something that cheap...
**I:** Well, good luck!

d
**I:** Good morning. I see you're looking at The Clothing Company website.
Are you OK to answer a couple of questions about it?
**C:** That's fine.
**I:** What are you looking for?
**C:** I'm looking for a new suit.
**I:** What is it for?
**C:** For work. I'm a teacher and have just got a new job.
**I:** Can I ask how much you are looking to spend?
**C:** 150 dollars.
**I:** Great, thanks.

1.33

a Are you wearing jeans?
Yes, I am./No, I'm not.
b Are you sitting next to a window?
Yes, I am./No, I'm not.
c Is your teacher standing up?
Yes, she is./No, she isn't.
d Is the traffic making a noise?
Yes, it is./No, it isn't.
e Are all of you wearing a watch?
Yes, we are./No, we're not.
f Are the birds singing outside?
Yes, they are./No, they're not.

1.34

Good evening. I'm Ross White and I'm standing outside the Kodak Theater in Hollywood. I'm waiting for the big stars to arrive for this year's Oscars ceremony. And here comes Emma Stone. She's wearing a beautiful dress. Oh, wow – there's Nicole Kidman. She's talking to the photographers. Oh, and what's she doing now? She's turning around. Hi, Nicole! Good luck! Oh, boy! She's looks fantastic. Leo DiCaprio's arriving now. He's wearing a black suit. Oh, he's so good-looking! And he's smiling at everyone.

1.35

a I'm waiting for the big stars.
b She's wearing a beautiful dress.
c She's turning around.
d He's wearing a black suit.
e He's smiling at everyone.

1.36

a Drive carefully. Don't be late.
b Smile! Say cheese!
c Don't worry! He's OK.
d Have a good time. Take care. Call me.

1.37

**Lauren:** Bye, Mom. Bye, Dad.
**Dad:** Drive carefully.
**Lauren:** Don't worry, Dad.
**Mom:** Have a good time in New York.
**Lauren:** Thanks, Mom.
**Dad:** Don't forget your phone.
**Lauren:** OK. My phone's in my bag.
**Mom:** Call us. Take care.
**Lauren:** OK. Bye. See you!

1.38

**Name:**
Rosie Gray
**Job:**
teacher

**Experience:**
Five years at Brilliant English Academy, Beijing, China.
Three years at Oxford School of English, Sao Paulo, Brazil.
1 year teacher training at ELF Institute, London, the UK.

**About:**
Smart and organized
Good with children
Strong leader

## Unit 3

1.39

**a**
I love sneakers. I have about ten pairs and I'm looking for more. I like to enter shoe stores to look at them. My wife hates shoe stores. She only has one pair of sneakers!
**b**
I have to say sorry to my husband. Romantic dinner? I go online and check out the sports scores. I want to know about my team, the New York Yankees, all the time. My husband doesn't like sports. He just goes online to watch funny cat videos!
**c**
We have two cars. I drive a normal car. It's a gray sedan. It's comfortable. My wife drives a new Ford Mustang. And she drives it very, very fast. I don't go in her car very often.

1.40

**a** Do you like shopping?
Yes, I do./No, I don't.
**b** Does your father do the housework?
Yes, he does./No, he doesn't.
**c** Do you think about chocolate all the time?
Yes, I do./No, I don't
**d** Does your mother work on weekends?
Yes, she does./No, she doesn't.
**e** Do you and your friends chat online?
Yes, we do./No, we don't.

1.43

**a** Running, walking,
Listening, talking.
**b** Eating, drinking,
Sleeping, thinking.
**c** Selling, buying,
Sailing, flying.

1.44

**a** I don't like The Beatles. Do you like them?
**b** I don't like Justin Bieber. Do you like him?
**c** I don't like Taylor Swift. Do you like her?
**d** I don't like Kanye West. Do you like him?
**e** I don't like Maroon 5. Do you like them?
**f** I don't like dance music. Do you like it?

1.46

**a**
**Ann:** What do you think of Pharrell Williams?
**Bob:** I think he's great.
**Ann:** I agree. I really like him.
**b**
**Fran:** What do you think of Coldplay?
**Salvatore:** I think they're terrible. What about you?
**Fran:** I don't agree. I think they're OK.
**c**
**Cathy:** What do you think of Emma Watson?
**Debra:** I think she's great. What about you?
**Cathy:** I think she's OK, but I prefer Jennifer Lawrence.
**d**
**Harry:** What do you think of Neymar?
**Isobel:** Who?
**Harry:** Neymar. He's a soccer player.
**Isobel:** I don't know. What do you think of him?
**Harry:** I think he's great.

## REVIEW A

1.49

**Officer:** Open your bag, please, sir.
**Man:** Yes, sure.
**Officer:** What's this?
**Man:** It's an iPad.
**Officer:** Mm. And what are these?
**Man:** They're tickets.
**Officer:** Tickets?
And what's this?
**Man:** It's a cell phone.
**Officer:** Ah, yes. What's this?
**Man:** It's a camera.
**Officer:** Oh, ... and what are these?
**Man:** They're tissues. I have a cold.
**Officer:** Fine. Thank you, sir.

1.50

**A** doctor, dentist,
**B** hairdresser, Portugal, Italy, camera, officer
**C** Brazil, Chinese, Japan

1.51

**(S = Shelly; J = Jeff)**
**S:** Hi, Jeff. It's me, Shelly.
**J:** Oh, hey, Shelly.
**S:** So, are you looking at the site?
**J:** Yes, I am.
**S:** And? Is there someone we could hire?
**J:** Well, Dan Evans looks good. I think he's 24.
**S:** Yes, but he only has one years' experience. And he likes sleeping!
**J:** Oh ...
**S:** What about Marnie?
**J:** Mmm. Maybe.
**S:** She's a teacher. And she likes working hard.
**J:** But she's British. Does she have a visa?
**S:** Good point. Okay, there's Juan. Where's he from?
**J:** He's from Mexico. But he likes traveling.
**S:** Let's give him a call.
**J:** OK. What's his number?
**S:** It's here. 011-52-55-37732.
**J:** OK, I'll call him and tell you how it goes.
**S:** Great.

## Unit 4

1.53

**a do**
do my homework
do the housework
do the shopping
do the laundry
do the dishes

**b make**
make a lot of noise
make breakfast
make long telephone calls
make the beds
make the decisions

1.54

**a** always
**b** usually
**c** often
**d** sometimes
**e** hardly ever
**f** never

1.56

**a** first, second, third
**b** seventh, sixth, second
**c** fifth, first, fourth
**d** tenth, twentieth, twelfth

1.59

**a** a quarter to nine in the evening - 8:45 p.m.
**b** six o'clock in the evening - 6:00 p.m.
**c** a quarter to seven at night - 6:45 p.m.
**d** six thirty in the morning - 6:30 a.m.
**e** a quarter to eight in the morning - 7:45 a.m.

1.60

**a** Something you never do on Sundays.
**b** Something you always do in the mornings.
**c** Something you usually do at 8:00 a.m.
**d** Something you always do on December 31.
**e** Something you sometimes do on Saturday nights.

1.62

**(M = Man; W = Woman)**
**M:** Are you going to the Festival this year?
**W:** Of course, I go every year.
What about you?
**M:** No. I don't like the festival any more. I'm going to the beach for a week instead.
**W:** Really? But it's fun. The music and the art is fantastic. I love it!
**M:** I don't like all the dance music. And there are too many people these days.
**W:** But what about the big fire at the end? That's pretty spectacular.
**M:** Sure, but I can watch that online.
**W:** Watch it online? No! That's terrible. I love dancing all night in the desert. And then, of course, cleaning up the site in the morning!

1.63

My favorite festival is Saint Patrick's Day. It takes place in downtown Dublin. It takes place in March and it runs for four days. On March 17 – the most important day – we have a big parade in the city. At the end of the parade, thousands of people do traditional Irish dancing together. It's fantastic! People wear green clothes and paint their faces green. We drink a lot of dark beer – that's Guinness, of course. And we listen to traditional Irish music in the bars. Ah, Irish people love a good party!

1.65

**a** What time do you open?
**b** We open at nine o'clock.
**c** What time does it open?
**d** What time does it close?
**e** What time do you close?
**f** We close at 5:30.
**g** We're closed on Sunday.

## Unit 5

1.67

**(I = Interviewer; P = Pam)**

**1**

**I:** Excuse me. I'm from a new sports store. Can I ask you some questions about water sports?
**P:** Sure.
**I:** What's your name?
**P:** It's Pam.
**I:** OK, Pam. Do you ever go swimming?
**P:** Oh, yes. I love swimming.
**I:** And when was the last time you went swimming?
**P:** Er, the last time I went swimming was ... in August. I was on vacation.
**I:** And do you ever go sailing?
**P:** No – I'd like to, but I don't know anyone with a boat.
**I:** OK. How about other water sports?
**P:** I sometimes go windsurfing.
**I:** When was the last time you went windsurfing?
**P:** I went windsurfing last summer with my friend. We were on vacation.
**I:** Great. Well, why don't you come to our store sometime? Here's the address.
**P:** Yeah, thanks.

**(I = Interviewer; S = Steven)**

**2**

**I:** Excuse me. I'm from a new sports store. Can I ask you some questions about water sports?
**S:** Water sports?
**I:** Yes, what's your name?
**S:** Steven Franklin-Phillips.
**I:** Ok, er, Steve. Do you ever go swimming?
**S:** Yes, yes, I go swimming a lot.
**I:** Oh. great. When was the last time you went swimming?
**S:** Yesterday!
**I:** OK, and do ever go sailing?
**S:** Yes, but not often.
**I:** When was the last time you went sailing?
**S:** I can't remember. A long time ago.
**I:** Do you ever do other water sports?
**S:** Yes, I love scuba diving.
**I:** Wow. When was the last time you went scuba diving?
**S:** Last year. I was on vacation in Mexico.
**I:** Great. Well, our new store is downtown ...

1.68

**a** Do you ever go swimming?
**b** When was the last time you went swimming?

1.70

**a** ask-asked
**b** chat-chatted
**c** finish-finished
**d** smile-smiled
**e** start-started

1.71

**a** go - went / do - did / send - sent
**b** hold - held / sell - sold / tell - told
**c** think - thought / catch - caught/ hear - heard
**d** take - took / break - broke/ speak - spoke
**e** tear - tore/ come - came / wear - wore
**f** read - read /say - said / give - gave

1.72

**a** went, did, sent
**b** held, sold, told
**c** thought, caught, heard
**d** took, broke, spoke
**e** tore, came, wore
**f** read, said, gave

1.73

**A: No extra syllables**
ask - asked
love - loved
stop - stopped
use - used
work - worked

**B: Extra syllable**
point - pointed
start - started
want - wanted

1.75

A man and woman went on vacation to the Indian Ocean. One day, they went on a boat with twenty other people and went scuba diving. The boat stopped in the middle of the ocean, and everyone went diving. After an hour, everyone returned to the boat, and the boat went back to the port. But the man and woman didn't return to the boat. When they finished diving, there was no boat. At first, they shouted, but no one heard them. They waited and waited for the boat to return, but eventually they realized they were alone. Suddenly, something moved near them under the water. Two weeks later, a fisherman found their camera.

1.77

**1** How's the weather?
**2** It's sunny.
**3** It's windy.
**4** It's cloudy.
**5** It's raining.
**6** It's snowing.
**7** It's foggy.

1.78

Hello, to everyone arriving on the SunTours flight from Houston. Unfortunately, we have a few problems here on the island... The hotel, the magnificent Beach House, has been doing some building work, but it ran out of money last month. So, it only has 23 rooms available right now. So, er, ... anyone want to share? Also, the beach was closed last week because of pollution. I don't know when, er, or if, it will open. There is a pool...? The airport is also shutting down for the weekend so there are no flights for 3 days. The last flight left at nine o'clock this morning. There are also only four taxis on the island. Please wait here. They are arriving soon. Thank you for choosing SunTours and I hope you have a wonderful vacation.

## Unit 6

1.81

**(P = Presenter; N = Nancy)**

**P:** Welcome to this week's edition of our podcast, Heroes.
Today we have the popular TV presenter Nancy B in our studio. Nancy, hello, and welcome.
**N:** Thank you. It's good to be here.
**P:** Nancy, who is your hero, and why?
**N:** My hero is Katie Spotz because she rowed across the Atlantic alone.
**P:** Alone?! Wow! That's amazing. How did she do it?
**N:** She was in a 19-foot wooden boat. And she's the youngest person to have done it. She's only 22!
**P:** She must have been scared.
**N:** I think she was a couple of times. When her steering broke, and when her GPS tracker caught fire. And she was scared of running out of food. The big waves made her nervous as well. But Katie is a very strong woman, and she made it through all of that. I know she was very happy about landing in Georgetown.
**P:** What about her family?
**N:** Well, actually, her family wasn't so worried about her. They know she's a good rower and her Dad spoke to her every day via a satellite phone to keep her going.
**P:** Do you think this is something you would be interested in doing?
**N:** Me? No! I'm very embarrassed to say that I'm not a great swimmer. But Katie has inspired me to take on more challenges. And as soon as Katie was finished she told me she was interested in new challenges. And that's why she's a hero for me.
**P:** That's great. And we're so happy you could come on and share this story. And thanks to all for listening to our Heroes podcast. Until next time.

1.82

**a** I'm worried about my future.
**b** I'm never angry with my friends.
**c** I'm scared of snakes.
**d** I'm not interested in modern art.
**e** I'm not embarrassed about my English.

1.84

**e** Syd Barrett was born in Cambridge.
**a** Syd met Roger Waters at school.
**g** Pink Floyd was formed in 1965.
**c** Syd Barrett left Pink Floyd.
**b** Syd recorded two solo albums.
**h** Syd walked from London to Cambridge.
**d** Syd started using the name 'Roger'.
**f** Syd died aged 60.

1.85

**a** Did you go to elementary school near here?
Yes, I did./No, I didn't.
**b** Did you walk to school?
Yes, I did./No, I didn't.
**c** Did you move when you were a child?
Yes, I did./No, I didn't.
**d** Did your father leave school at sixteen?
Yes, he did./No, he didn't.
**e** Did your mother study English at school?
Yes, she did./No, she didn't.
**f** Did your parents go to college?
Yes, they did./No, they didn't.

1.86

**A** know - knew /mean - meant / tear - tore
speak - spoke / think - thought
**B** break - broke / fly - flew / spend - spent
teach - taught / wear - wore

1.87

knew - flew
meant - spent
tore - wore
spoke - broke
thought - taught

1.88

**(M = Man; L = Laura)**

**M:** I don't know where to go on vacation this year. Where did you go for your last summer vacation?
**L:** I went to the beach – to Miami, in Florida.
**M:** Oh, wow. When did you go there?
**L:** Mm, in July.
**M:** Nice. Who did you go with?
**L:** I went alone. I always go on vacation alone.
**M:** Oh, OK ... How did you get there?
**L:** I went by plane and by car. I flew from Chicago to Orlando, and then I drove from Orlando to Miami. There's a really good highway.
**M:** Great. Where did you stay?
**L:** In a hotel – the Hurricane Hotel. Do you know it?
**M:** No – what's it like?
**L:** Fantastic. The rooms are wonderful. And it's near the beach.
**M:** Mm, you are lucky. How long did you stay?
**L:** Just two weeks, unfortunately.
**M:** Oh, well. So what did you do all day?
**L:** I went to the beach, of course – you can do everything there. I tried kitesurfing – it's amazing.
**M:** Wow – and what did you do in the evening?
**L:** I went out to the bars and clubs. There's a lot to do in Miami.
**M:** Mm, and did you meet anyone nice?
**L:** Well, yes, I did, actually. He's a windsurfing instructor, and the first time we went out ...

1.91

**a** I'm bored. Why don't you go out with your friends?
**b** I'm hungry. Why don't you have a snack?
**c** I'm tired. Me, too. Let's stream a movie tonight.
**d** I'm hungry. Why don't you have an early lunch?
**e** I'm thirsty. Me, too. Let's have coffee.
**f** I'm bored. Why don't you play on your computer?

## REVIEW B

1.92

**A** August, nervous, worried, always, fishing, surfing
**B** windsurfing, terrible, usually
**C** embarrassed, excited, November, October, September

1.94

This is the news for Tuesday, July 4. This morning, actor and writer David Walliams walked into the ocean at Dover in the south of England. At 5:30 a.m., David started his swim across the English Channel. Greg Whyte, his trainer, followed him in a boat, and gave him bananas and chocolate. David Walliams swam 34 kilometers from Dover to Calais, in France. The swim took 10 hours and 30 minutes. The ocean was cold – 15 degrees centigrade, but David didn't have any problems and arrived in Calais at 4:00 p.m. He was very happy to finish so quickly. David made more than $2 million for the charity Sport Relief. The money goes to help poor people all over the world.

## Unit 7

2.03

**a** bread
**b** mango
**c** garlic
**d** cheese

2.04

a Are there any mushrooms in picture *d*?
Yes, there are./No, there aren't.
b Is there any cheese in picture *b*?
Yes, there is./No, there isn't.
c Are there any eggs in picture *b*?
Yes, there are./No, there aren't.
d Is there any pasta in picture *d*?
Yes, there is./No, there isn't.

2.06

**(R = Ricardo; G = Gina)**
**R:** What are you doing?
**G:** I'm looking at these diets.
**R:** Oh, I need to lose weight. Which diet is this one?
**G:** It's the Paleo diet.
**R:** Paleo diet? What's that?
**G:** It's a great diet. You can eat meat.
**R:** And potatoes? I love potatoes.
**G:** No, no potatoes on the Paleo diet. You can eat potatoes on the Vegan Special diet. And pasta and bread.
**R:** That sounds good. What about bananas?
**G:** Yes, you can eat bananas. And you can eat bananas on the Sugar Busters diet. As long as they are green!
**R:** Green? Who eats green bananas ...? I think my new diet is going to be the Paleo diet.
**G:** Good luck!

2.07

a How much bread is there?
There isn't much.
b How many eggs are there?
There are a lot.
c How many lemons are there?
There aren't any.
d How much meat is there?
There isn't much.
e How much milk is there?
There isn't any.
f How many peppers are there?
There aren't many.

2.08

We had a great dinner last weekend. It was my friend's 21st birthday, and the whole family went out. We had dinner in an Italian restaurant. It's called Mario's, and they make fantastic pizzas. There were eight of us. I sat next to Sofia. We ate a big cheese pizza. Everyone ate pizza. The restaurant made my friend a special birthday cake, and we all sang "Happy Birthday." The cake was delicious, and we had some wine, too. I think we stayed in the restaurant for almost three hours. It was a really fun evening.

2.09

**(S = Server; C = Customer)**
**S:** Next, please!
**C:** I'd like a ham and cheese sandwich, please.
**S:** Would you like brown bread or white bread, butter or mayonnaise, mustard or ketchup?
**C:** Er, I'd like just a ham and cheese sandwich.
**S:** Yes, I know you'd like a ham and cheese sandwich. But would you like brown bread or white bread, butter ...?
**C:** Sorry. Could you speak more slowly, please?
**S:** Sorry. Let's start again. Would you like white or brown bread?
**C:** Brown bread, please.
**S:** Would you like butter or mayonnaise?
**C:** Butter, please.
**S:** Would you like mustard or ketchup?
**C:** Mustard, please.
**S:** Would you like something to drink?
**C:** Er, something to drink?
**S:** Yes ... orange juice, water, coffee...
**C:** No, thanks.
**S:** Okay. That's twelve dollars, please.

## Unit 8

2.12

She went to New York to see a show. She saw a homeless man. She decided to give some money. Frankie created an Internet page. She raised $2,500 for having a hair cut. Frankie gave the money to charity.

2.13

a I bought some new clothes last weekend.
b I never save money. I always spend all my money.
c I never use my credit card to buy things online.
d I donate money to charity once a year.
e I always pay my bills on time.

2.14

**short adjectives:**
bigger/cleaner/faster/happier/older/richer
**long adjectives:**
more beautiful/more important
**irregular forms:**
better

2.15

a I'm taller than Karl.
b I'm older than Terri.
c My typing is worse than Gina's.
d My cell phone is smaller than Eddie's.
e My apartment is farther from the office than Alan's.
f My computer was more expensive than Kerry's.

2.17

a One million, two hundred and fifty thousand, six hundred and twenty dollars
b Six hundred and twelve thousand dollars
c Three million, eight hundred and seventy-seven thousand, one hundred and eighty dollars
d Sixty-five thousand, two hundred and eight dollars

2.18

1 One of the world's most expensive watches is by Patek Phillipe. It's made of titanium and is worth three million, eight hundred and seventy-seven thousand, one hundred and eighty dollars.
2 One of the most valuable pair of jeans is an original pair of 115-year old Levis. A collector bought them for sixty-five thousand, two hundred and eight dollars.
3 A very valuable dress is the one worn by the actor Marilyn Monroe when she sang Happy Birthday, Mr President to JF Kennedy in 1962. A collector bought the dress for one million, two hundred and fifty thousand, six hundred and twenty dollars.
4 A very valuable pair of shoes is a pair worn by the character Dorothy in the famous movie *The Wizard of Oz*. There are four pairs and one pair is in a museum in Washington. This pair was bought for six hundred and twelve thousand dollars.

2.19

a Who's the youngest?
b Who's the oldest?
c Who's the most interesting?
d Who's the luckiest?
e Who's the worst driver?
f Who's the best cook?

2.23

**a**
This phone is amazing! It's the best phone ever! So much better than my old phone. It has better apps, a nicer screen, and the camera takes the most amazing photos. It's great value for money. Buy it now and you can save 15%.
**b**
This is the worst phone. It's more expensive than other phones, but itn't better. It's slower than the GrU13 and the screen is smaller. I'm glad I used my credit card so I can get my money back. Save your money and buy something else.

## Unit 9

2.24

It's another *Celebrity Secrets* podcast. This time we're talking about the hidden talents of some famous people. First up we have jam-maker. Yes, that's right – pop star Taylor Swift can make delicious homemade jam. She gives it out as gifts to her closest friends. Next, did you know that singer Justin Bieber can complete a Rubik's cube in about a minute and a half. Now, the world record is 6 seconds, but still ... Justin can do it a lot quicker than most people. It's taken me 10 years and I STILL can't complete it! And what about actor Colin Farrell? Well, the handsome Irishman started out as dancer. Yes, Colin can do country and line dancing! That's something I'd like to see. And finally, Shakira has everything – she's beautiful and talented and she can speak Spanish, English, Italian, Arabic, and Portuguese. Wow. Five languages!

2.25

a Can you make jam?
Yes, I can./No, I can't.
b Can your father dance?
Yes, he can./No, he can't.
c Can you swim?
Yes, I can./No, I can't.
d Can you speak five languages?
Yes, I can./No, I can't.
e Can your mother ride a horse?
Yes, she can./No, she can't.
f Can your parents ski?
Yes, they can./No, they can't.

2.27

a I eat my food very slowly.
b I drive my car pretty fast.
c I play the guitar very badly.
d I spend my money very carefully.
e I play the drums very loudly.
f I don't eat my soup very quietly.
g I do my homework very happily.
h I don't speak English very well.

2.29

a She travels every month.
b She sleeps eight hours a night.
c She practices eight hours a day.
d She eats nuts three times a day.
e She wants to publish a book every two years.
f Her mother worked sixty hours a week.

2.30

1 three times a day
2 every day
3 twice a week
4 every two weeks
5 once a month
6 four times a year

2.31

a How often do you travel?
b How often do you buy new shoes?
c How often do you call your family?

2.32

a confident
3 - You are very sure of yourself.
b generous
1 - You give a lot of time and/or money to people.
c selfish
5 - You don't think about other people.
d sensible
6 - You never do stupid things.
e serious
4 - You think about things and don't laugh much.
f shy
2 - You are nervous about meeting people.

2.34

a 2: I have a bad back.
b 4: I don't have time.
c 1: I'm really tired.
d 5: I have a cold.
e 6: I have a headache.
f 3: I don't have any money.

2.37

a **(W = Woman; M = Man)**
**1**
**W:** This is a good song, isn't it?
**M:** It is. I can sing this song.
**W:** Can you? Are you a good singer?
**M:** I can sing very well. Listen ...[sings very badly]
**W:** Stop! STOP, PLEASE! That's terrible. I think you can sing ...VERY badly.
**2**
**W:** Ooh, I can dance to this music.
**M:** Really? Okay, go on then.
**W:** I will ... hey, where are you going?
**M:** I'm sorry, but you can't dance AT ALL. So, I'm pretending I don't know you ...
**3**
**W:** Do you know most men think they can drive well?
**M:** I know, but I can drive perfectly. Look I'm ...
**W:** WATCH OUT! [crash]
**M:** Okay, maybe I can't drive that well ...
**W:** You're driving carelessly! I'm taking the bus ...

## REVIEW C

2.38

A lemon, badly, boring
B carefully, sandwiches, happily, strawberries
C banana, potato, tomato

2.40

**(R = Receptionist; Lara)**
**R:** Luigi's. Can I help you?
**L:** Yes, I'd like to make a reservation, please.
**R:** Of course. What day?
**L:** Friday, August 15.
**R:** Is that for lunch or dinner?
**L:** Dinner.
**R:** I'm sorry. We have tables for lunch, but there aren't any tables for dinner on the 15th. There's a big party that night.
**L:** Oh. It's my birthday.
**R:** Would you like a different day?
**L:** What about Saturday – Saturday, August 16th?
**R:** For dinner?
**L:** Yes.
**R:** Yes. We have some tables for dinner on Saturday.
**L:** Great.
**R:** How many people?
**L:** Six. Do you have a window table?
**R:** Excuse me?
**L:** Do you have a table near the window with a view of the park?
**R:** Certainly. What time would you like, seven thirty or nine o'clock?
**L:** Er, nine, I think.
**R:** And what's your name?
**L:** Lara Gluck.
**R:** Can you spell that, please?
**L:** L-A-R-A G-L-U-C-K.
**R:** OK. That's a window table for six people at 9:00 p.m. on Saturday, August 16th.
**L:** Thanks. Is there a dress code?
**R:** Yes. No jeans, and we ask men to wear a jacket.
**L:** OK. Oh, and can I pay by credit card?
**R:** Yes, that's no problem. See you Saturday.

## Unit 10

2.41

a How many TVs do you have in your house?
b How many hours of TV do you watch every day?
c When do you usually turn on the TV? When do you turn it off?
d How many different channels can you get on your TV?
e What's your favorite TV show?
f What's on TV this evening?

2.42

a **(W = Woman; M = Man)**
1
**W:** Next question. On the border of which two South American countries can you find the Iguaçu Falls?
**M:** Oh. Um. Mm. I know this one. Is it Argentina and Chile? No – Argentina and Brazil.
**W:** Is that your final answer?
**M:** Yes.
**W:** Are you sure?
**M:** Mm, yes.
**W:** t's the correct answer – YOU JUST WON $125,000!
2
Police arrested two men after they attempted to rob a bank in downtown Atlanta this morning.
The men were armed, but no one was hurt.
3
**W:** Oh, hello, Mr. Jones. How are you doing?
**M:** Good. Did you hear about Tony Cortez?
**W:** No, what?
**M:** Well, I heard he's going to get married to ... Maria Gomez.
**W:** Maria Gomez – no!
4
**W:** Well, Michael, you've had a very successful career in the movie business. Did you always want to be a movie star?
**M:** Not exactly. I grew up on a farm in the Midwest, and when I was a young boy, all I wanted to be was a farmer like my dad.
**W:** So what made you change your mind?
**M:** Well, it was ...
5
The shark is the king of the ocean. It fills people with fear.
But that's not the whole story.
Yes, some kinds of shark are dangerous, but most of them are harmless and shy.
Take the Spotted White Shark ...
6
**W:** This is The Big Brother Show. The nominations for eviction are Diane ...
**M:** Oh ... I knew it ...
**W:** And ... Clyde!

2.45

a I want to travel around the world.
b I want to live in a different country.
c I'd like to have a lot of children.
d I wouldn't like to be famous.
e I hope to retire before I'm sixty.

2.46

**(I = Interviewer; L = Lola)**
**I:** Lola, congratulations!
**L:** Thanks! I can't believe it!
**I:** What's the first thing you're going to do now you have won *Who's Got Talent*?
**L:** I'm going to have a big party! I want to thank all my family and friends.
**I:** Ah. What are you going to do with the money?
**L:** I'm going to buy a house for my mom.
**I:** Oh, that's great. Which of the *Who's Got Talent*? finalists are you going to see again?
**L:** There are some people I'd like to see again, but I'm not going to see Josh or Sammy – they were mean to me.
**I:** Oh, that's a shame .... But what about Eddie? You became really good friends on the show. Are you going to see Eddie again?
**L:** Yes, of course we're going to see each other. I miss him already!
**I:** Finally, Lola, what are your plans for the future?
**L:** Well, first I'm going to go out and spend some money. Then I want to start my singing career. I'm going to record some songs. I'd also like to go on tour.
**I:** Oh, well, good luck!

2.47

a Is she going to have a big party?
Yes, she is./No, she isn't.
b Is she going to buy a house for her mom?
Yes, she is./No, she isn't.
c Is she going to see Josh and Sammy?
Yes, she is./No, she isn't.
d Is she going to see Eddie?
Yes, she is./No, she isn't.
e Is she going to go out and spend some money?
Yes, she is./No, she isn't.
f Is she going to record some songs?
Yes, she is./No, she isn't.

2.48

**A**
What do you want to do?
Where do you want to go?
Who do you want to see?
I don't want to come.
**B**
What are you going to do?
Where are you going to go?
Who are you going to see?
I'm not going to come.

2.49

**(I = Interviewer; J = Juliet)**
**I:** OK, Juliet. So, what's your favorite TV show?
**J:** My favorite TV show? The Big Bang Theory.
**I:** What kind of a show is it?
**J:** It's a comedy.
**I:** Who are the main characters?
**J:** There are five main characters – Leonard, Sheldon, Penny, er, and then there's Howard. And of course, Raj. They all live in California and are friends. And they are all geeks – apart from Penny!
**I:** What's it about?
**J:** It's about their lives. Four of them work together at Caltech and there are lot of science jokes.
**I:** Who's your favorite character?
**J:** Mm. I like Penny. She's so smart!
**I:** When is it on?
**J:** It's on Thursday at 8.
**I:** Did you see it last Thursday?
**J:** Yes, of course.
**I:** What happened?
**J:** It was SO funny. Raj moved into Leonard's apartment. It didn't go well.
**I:** Why do you like it?
**J:** I like the humor – I'm a bit of a geek myself and I know plenty of guys like Sheldon and Leonard! Anyway, what's your favorite show?
**I:** Er, Game of Thrones?

2.50

**Ruby:** What's on TV tonight?
**Joe:** Nothing.
**Ruby:** Should we go out?
**Joe:** Good idea. Let's go to the movies.
**Ruby:** OK. What's playing?
**Joe:** I don't know.
**Ruby:** Just a minute – I'll look online. ... Oh, great. *Pirates of the Caribbean*.
**Joe:** What, again? It's so old.
**Ruby:** Should I book tickets?
**Joe:** No. I don't want to see it again. Let's stream a movie.
**Ruby:** OK. Should I choose a movie?
**Joe:** No, it's OK – I'll choose. I'd like to see a movie without Johnny Depp in it.

2.52

a Coming this fall is *Explorer*, TBC's new reality show. Watch as 8 contestants battle it out in the jungles of South America, and try to find the hidden treasure.
b On next is another episode of our hit reality TV show, *Fire! Fire!*, as we follow a team of firefighters as they work and play. Tonight, a big fire at the port tests the fire crew.
c Coming soon, Sally, Marcy, Phoenix and Rita – yes, the famous Talbot family in our new show, *Life With The Talbots*. We follow the actors, and sisters, as they live, work and fight in Hollywood.
d Up next, the final episode of the award-winning show, *Move!* Which dancer will win first prize. Jolie or Stan? Watch and get ready to vote.
e Next week, a new show. Get *There First* follows three teams as they race across Asia – by car, train, by bus, by elephant ...? Which team will win? Watch Tuesday at 7.

## Unit 11

2.54

1 **Steve**
I love shopping. I've been to Hong Kong, and there are fantastic stores there. But my favorite place to shop is New York City. It's amazing.
2 **Brad**
I don't like cities – there are too many cars and people everywhere. I love going to wild places. I've been to the Amazon – that was amazing. I love deserts, but I haven't been to the Sahara yet. That's my next trip.
3 **Rachel**
I enjoy walking. So I've been to the Rocky Mountains and the North Island in New Zealand. I also love historical places. I've been to Petra in Jordan and the Great Wall of China. One day, I'd like to visit Tikal in Guatemala.

2.55

a I've been to New York.
b He's been to Hawaii.
c I haven't been to Tikal.
d He hasn't been to Petra.

2.56

a Have you ever been to Machu Picchu?
Yes, I have./No, I haven't.
b Has your father ever been to California?
Yes, he has./No, he hasn't.
c Have you ever been to a big rock concert?
Yes, I have./No, I haven't.
d Has your mother even been to a baseball game?
Yes, she has./No, she hasn't.
e Have you and your family ever been to Chile?
Yes, we have. No, we haven't.

2.57

1 worked
2 bought
3 done
4 met
5 swum
6 driven

2.58

**A**

| | | |
|---|---|---|
| break | broke | broken |
| speak | spoke | spoken |
| do | did | done |
| swim | swam | swum |

**B**

| | | |
|---|---|---|
| shake | shook | shaken |
| take | took | taken |
| fly | flew | flown |
| know | knew | known |

**c**

| | | |
|---|---|---|
| give | gave | given |
| drive | drove | driven |
| say | said | said |
| read | read | read |

2.60

**(W = Winnie; R = Rick)**

**W:** Hello.
**R:** Hi, Winnie!
**W:** Rick! ...
**R:** How are you doing, Winnie?
**W:** I'm good. Hey, where are you?
**R:** In Ecuador.
**W:** Ecuador? Amazing. How's it going?
**R:** Great. I'm enjoying my time here. I've seen a lot of South America.
**W:** Where have you been?
**R:** Argentina, Chile, Peru, Ecuador ... I've driven 12,000 kilometers in the last six months.
**W:** 12,000 kilometers! What's the best place you've been to?
**R:** I've seen so many beautiful places – but I think Patagonia was the best.
**W:** Have you been to Brazil?
**R:** Yeah, I have.
**W:** When did you go?
**R:** In February. I went to the Carnival in Rio.
**W:** Awesome!
**R:** Yeah, I met some great people in Rio. We had parties on the beach. It was really good fun.
**W:** What about the people on the trips?
**R:** Well, I've had a few problems.
**W:** Oh, no. What happened?
**R:** Well, one friend lost her passport. And another got sick – I brought him to the hospital.
**W:** Ah. Have you had any problems?
**R:** No, no. I haven't had any accidents.
**W:** Oh, good.
**R:** But ... I had a few problems with the police.
**W:** Really? What happened?
**R:** Oh, it's a long story – I'll write you.
**W:** OK. Have you met any nice people?
**R:** Yes – a lot of great people. I met a fantastic woman last month in Peru.
Her name's Ana and ...
**W:** Really? Tell me more. Rick? RICK? ... Oh, he's gone.

2.61

**a** He's seen a lot of South America.
**b** He's driven 12,000 kilometers.
**c** He's been to Brazil.
**d** He hasn't had any accidents.
**e** He's had a few problems with the police.
**f** He's met a lot of great people.

2.63

**a** Have you ever been to Cuba?
When did you go?
Who did you go with?
**b** Have you ever moved?
When did you move?
Where did you move to?
**c** Have you ever lost your credit card?
When did you lose it?
What did you do?
**d** Have you ever won a prize?
What did you win?
When did you win it?
**e** Have you ever seen a Tom Hanks movie?
What did you see it?
Which one did you see?

2.64

My oldest friend is Brett. We first met at school – high school. We were fifteen or sixteen years old – I can't remember exactly. We became friends because we laugh at the same things. Brett is very funny. Now he's a doctor. He's married and he lives in London. I see him a few times a year. The last time I saw him was on his birthday. We went out for dinner. His wife and my girlfriend get along really well. My best memory of Brett is a vacation we took together in the USA. We were twenty-three, and it was the year we finished college. We drove from Chicago to Los Angeles. It was fantastic.

## Unit 12

2.68

**a** **Stelvio** - The drive is in Italy.
**b** **Big Sur** - The drive is in the USA.
**c** **Stelvio** -The road is fifteen miles long.
**d** **Stelvio** - There are sixty bends on the road.
**e** **Big Sur** - You can see a lighthouse.
**f** **Big Sur** - You can visit Carmel.

2.69

**a** I go down the stairs.
**b** I go out of my apartment.
**c** I go across the street.
**d** I go along the river.
**e** I go past some stores.
**f** I go up a hill.
**g** I go through the park.
**h** I go over a bridge.
**i** I go into my office.

2.70

**a** Where do you start from?
**b** Who do you travel with?
**c** What do you talk about?
**d** What kind of music do you listen to?
**e** What kind of scenery do you go through?
**f** What kind of buildings do you go past?

2.72

**a** car/start/part
**b** world/first/turn
**c** small/saw/walk
**d** blue/two/through

2.73

**(I = Interviewer; K = Kelly)**

**I:** Welcome to *Amazing Journeys*. Today's show is about a man who has traveled around the world by bicycle. Kelly, what can you tell us about Heinz Stücke?
**K:** Well, Heinz Stücke has actually been around the world ten times by bicycle.
**I:** Ten times?! When did he start his journey?
**K:** He started his journey in 1962. He left Germany when he was twenty-two years old. At first, he planned to travel only for a few years.
**I:** What happened?
**K:** Well, he forgot to stop.
**I:** How many countries has he visited?
**K:** Two hundred and eleven countries. He's filled fifteen passports.
**I:** Fifteen passports! And what kind of bicycle does he have?
**K:** It's a big, heavy bicycle – it weights twenty-five kilos. He has very strong legs!
**I:** I can imagine. Where does he sleep?
**K:** He usually sleeps in a tent.
**I:** And how does he make money?
**K:** He sells postcards of his trip.
**I:** I see. Where is he now?
**K:** Right now, he's riding along the west coast of Nicaragua.
**I:** So, when is he going to finish his ride?
**K:** I don't know. Maybe never.

2.75

**a** trees, forest, waterfall, bridge - 3
**b** desert, sand, tree - 4
**c** ocean, sand, rocks, beach, cliffs - 2
**d** fields, grass, hills, mountains, snow - 1

2.76

Last spring I went to Arizona, one of my favorite places in the USA.
I went with my friend, Julia. We had a little Corvette. I drove and Julia read the map. I can't read maps. One day we decided to drive from Phoenix to Tucson. We left Phoenix in the morning and it was already sunny and hot. We drove through desert and hills. Arizona is so beautiful. We stopped in a small town in the desert. We visited an old church and bought some jewelry. Then we continued our drive and arrived in Tucson in the afternoon. Tucson is a great place to visit. We ate fantastic Mexican food in a café called the Café Poca Cosa.

2.77

**a** Go down Forty-First Street. - 3
**b** Across from the church. - 7
**c** Take the second street on the left. - 5
**d** Go straight. - 6
**e** There's a motel on the left. - 8
**f** Go to the end of Washington Avenue. - 4
**g** Turn right. - 2
**h** Turn left. - 1

2.78

**(W = Woman; M = Man)**

**a**
**W:** Hi, where are you?
**M:** I'm at the station.
**W:** OK. Turn left and go down Lincoln Avenue. Take the third street on the right. That's 32nd Street.
**M:** OK.
**W:** We live across from the church.
**M:** OK. See you in ten minutes.
**b**
**M:** Hello?
**W:** Hi, I'm at the station.
**M:** OK. Turn left and take the first street on the right. That's 34th Street.
**W:** OK.
**M:** There's a bar on the left. We're there.
**W:** Great. Get me a beer.
**c**
**W:** Hello?
**M:** Hello. I'm lost.
**W:** Where are you?
**M:** At the station.
**W:** OK. Turn right onto Lincoln Avenue and go down the street. Then turn left onto 35th Street.
**M:** OK.
**W:** Go to the end of 35th Street and turn right onto Kennedy Avenue. There's a bank on the left and we live across the street, at number 3603.
**M:** OK, thanks. See you soon.

2.79

**(W = Woman; M = Man)**

**M:** Hi, I'm at the station.
**W:** OK. Turn right onto Lincoln Avenue. Take the second street on the left. That's Thirty-Sixth Street.
**M:** OK.
**W:** Go down Thirty-Sixth Street and take the first street on the left.
**M:** OK.
**W:** There's a movie theater on the left and our house is across the street.
**M:** Great. See you soon.

2.80

It's very easy to get there. From here, drive over the City Creek Bridge. Go along Main Street until you get to the junction with South Street. Turn right here and carry on down South Street. Take the second right, across from the park. Turn left at the traffic circle, then take a sharp left and it's on your left.

## REVIEW D

2.81

**A** desert, mountain, channel, chicken
**B** waterfall, comedy
**C** across, along, cartoon, dessert
**D** adventure, tomato

2.83

**(I = Interviewer; S = Shawna Tucker)**

**I:** Welcome to another episode of our podcast! Over the last few weeks we've been talking about inspiring women. Last week we were talking about Malala – this week, we're talking to someone who has been inspired by Malala. Welcome, Shawna Tucker.
**S:** Hi, thanks for having me today.
**I:** It's great to have you here. So, tell me about you and Malala.
**S:** Well, I heard about Malala's story, and it inspired us to do something for children.
So, me and my husband, John, started Blind Hope last year to help blind children in other countries.
**I:** And two weeks ago, something fantastic happened. Tell us about it.
**S:** Yes. Someone gave $1 million to Blind Hope. I can't say who gave us the money, but it will help a lot.
**I:** And now you're organizing a very special trip to Kenya.
**S:** Yes, that's right. We'd like to help blind children all around the world, and we're starting in Kenya. Blind Hope is going to use some of the money to open a school there.
**I:** And now, Shawna, I believe you are looking for people from this area who want to go to Kenya next year.
**S:** Yes. I'd like to find twelve people to help build the school with me.
**I:** What sort of people?
**S:** Well, we're looking for people who are friendly, confident, and who can work well with other people. We don't want people who only want to have a good time and travel. We want sensible people – this is a serious job. And its hard work. You need to be full of energy. It isn't a vacation.
**I:** I see. And what are Blind Hope's plans for the future, Shawna?
**S:** Blind Hope has big plans. We hope to build one school in a different country every year.
**I:** Good luck, Shawna. It's a great plan.
**S:** Thank you!

# Phonetic symbols

## Vowels

| | | |
|---|---|---|
| /ɪ/ | **fish** | /fɪʃ/ |
| /i/ | **bean** | /bin/ |
| /ʊ/ | **foot** | /fʊt/ |
| /u/ | **shoe** | /ʃu/ |
| /e/ | **egg** | /eg/ |
| /ə/ | **about** | /əˈbaʊt/ |
| /ɜr/ | **word** | /wɜrd/ |
| /ɔ/ | **talk** | /tɔk/ |
| /æ/ | **back** | /bæk/ |
| /ʌ/ | **bus** | /bʌs/ |
| /ɑ/ | **father** | /ˈfɑðər/ |

## Diphthongs

| | | |
|---|---|---|
| /eɪ/ | **face** | /feɪs/ |
| /ɔɪ/ | **boy** | /bɔɪ/ |
| /oʊ/ | **nose** | /noʊz/ |
| /aɪ/ | **eye** | /aɪ/ |
| /aʊ/ | **mouth** | /maʊθ/ |

## Consonants

| | | |
|---|---|---|
| /p/ | **pen** | /pen/ |
| /b/ | **bag** | /bæg/ |
| /t/ | **tea** | /ti/ |
| /d/ | **dog** | /dɔg/ |
| /tʃ/ | **chair** | /tʃer/ |
| /dʒ/ | **jazz** | /dʒæz/ |
| /k/ | **cake** | /keɪk/ |
| /g/ | **girl** | /gɜrl/ |
| /f/ | **staff** | /stæf/ |
| /v/ | **verb** | /vɜrb/ |
| /θ/ | **thing** | /θɪŋ/ |
| /ð/ | **these** | /ðiz/ |
| /s/ | **snake** | /sneɪk/ |
| /z/ | **zoo** | /zu/ |
| /ʃ/ | **shine** | /ʃaɪn/ |
| /ʒ/ | **measure** | /ˈmeʒər/ |
| /m/ | **map** | /mæp/ |
| /n/ | **name** | /neɪm/ |
| /ŋ/ | **ring** | /rɪŋ/ |
| /h/ | **house** | /haʊs/ |
| /l/ | **leg** | /leg/ |
| /r/ | **road** | /roʊd/ |
| /w/ | **wine** | /waɪn/ |
| /j/ | **yes** | /jes/ |

## Stress

Word stress is shown by underlining the stressed syllable:
*water, amazing, Japanese.*

## Letters of the alphabet

| /eɪ/ | /i/ | /e/ | /aɪ/ | /oʊ/ | /u/ | /ɑ/ |
|---|---|---|---|---|---|---|
| Aa | Bb | Ff | Ii | Oo | Qq | Rr |
| Hh | Cc | Ll | Yy | | Uu | |
| Jj | Dd | Mm | | | Ww | |
| Kk | Ee | Nn | | | | |
| | Gg | Ss | | | | |
| | Pp | Xx | | | | |
| | Tt | | | | | |
| | Vv | | | | | |
| | Zz | | | | | |

# Irregular verbs

| Infinitive | Simple past | Past participle |
|---|---|---|
| be | was/were | been |
| beat | beat | beaten |
| become | became | become |
| begin | began | begun |
| bend | bent | bent |
| bet | bet | bet |
| bite | bit | bitten |
| blow | blew | blown |
| break | broke | broken |
| bring | brought | brought |
| build | built | built |
| burst | burst | burst |
| buy | bought | bought |
| can | could | (been able) |
| catch | caught | caught |
| choose | chose | chosen |
| come | came | come |
| cost | cost | cost |
| cut | cut | cut |
| deal | dealt | dealt |
| dig | dug | dug |
| do | did | done |
| draw | drew | drawn |
| drink | drank | drunk |
| drive | drove | driven |
| eat | ate | eaten |
| fall | fell | fallen |
| feed | fed | fed |
| feel | felt | felt |
| fight | fought | fought |
| find | found | found |
| fly | flew | flown |
| forget | forgot | forgotten |
| forgive | forgave | forgiven |
| freeze | froze | frozen |
| get | got | gotten |
| give | gave | given |
| go | went | gone/been |
| grow | grew | grown |
| hang | hung/hanged | hung/hanged |
| have | had | had |
| hear | heard | heard |
| hide | hid | hidden |
| hit | hit | hit |
| hold | held | held |
| hurt | hurt | hurt |
| keep | kept | kept |
| know | knew | known |
| lay | laid | laid |
| lead | led | led |
| leave | left | left |
| lend | lent | lent |
| let | let | let |
| lie | lay | lain |
| lose | lost | lost |
| make | made | made |
| mean | meant | meant |

| Infinitive | Simple past | Past participle |
|---|---|---|
| meet | met | met |
| must | had to | (had to) |
| pay | paid | paid |
| put | put | put |
| read | read | read |
| ride | rode | ridden |
| ring | rang | rung |
| rise | rose | risen |
| run | ran | run |
| say | said | said |
| see | saw | seen |
| sell | sold | sold |
| send | sent | sent |
| set | set | set |
| shake | shook | shaken |
| shine | shone | shone |
| shoot | shot | shot |
| show | showed | shown |
| shrink | shrank | shrunk |
| shut | shut | shut |
| sing | sang | sung |
| sink | sank | sunk |
| sit | sat | sat |
| sleep | slept | slept |
| slide | slid | slid |
| speak | spoke | spoken |
| spend | spent | spent |
| split | split | split |
| spread | spread | spread |
| stand | stood | stood |
| steal | stole | stolen |
| stick | stuck | stuck |
| swear | swore | sworn |
| swell | swelled | swollen/swelled |
| swim | swam | swum |
| take | took | taken |
| teach | taught | taught |
| tear | tore | torn |
| tell | told | told |
| think | thought | thought |
| throw | threw | thrown |
| understand | understood | understood |
| wake | woke | woken |
| wear | wore | worn |
| win | won | won |
| write | wrote | written |

Macmillan Education

Companies and representatives throughout the world
American Inside Out Evolution. Student's Book Elementary

D.R. © Macmillan Publishers, S.A. de C.V., 2017
Text D.R. © Sue Kay and Vaughan Jones, 2017
Adapted by Peter Maggs and Catherine Smith / The Content Station team: Simon Campbell, George Wells and Catherine Gray
Macmillan is a registered trademark.
First edition published 2017

ISBN 978-607-473-647-2

Based on New American Inside Out Student's Book Elementary
D.R. © Macmillan Publishers, S.A. de C.V. 2008
Published under license from Macmillan Publishers Ltd.



Editorial Manager: Patricia Muradas
Editorial Operations Coordinator: Veronica Teodorov Ferreira
Editor: Cintia Zaitune
Concept design: Martha Tadaieski
Page make-up: The Content Station
Illustration: Karen Ahlschläger pp13, 25, 41, 47, 49, 63, 68, 69, 74, 79, 87, 91 ; Gustavo Gialuca pp12, 18, 34, 40, 46,56, 62, 68, 78, 84, 90
Graphic Production: Kelly Gobbo
Photographic research: The Content Station
Cover concept and design: Jean Aranha
Cover photo: Clinweaver | Dreamstime

The authors and publishers would like to thank the following for permission to reproduce their photographs:
**Dreamstime** / Rosshelen p8(t), Dreamstime / Rafaelpacheco p8 (Brazil), Dreamstime / Marcus Karlsson p8 (Germany), Dreamstime / Thomaspajot p8 (Italy), Dreamstime / Steve Allen p8 (Mexico), Dreamstime / Adrian Matthiassen p8 (Australia), Dreamstime / Paul Cowan p8 (Spain), Dreamstime / Rawpixelimages p8 (China), Dreamstime / Denisismagilov p8 (Japan), Dreamstime / Mustafa Sandikci p9(ta), Dreamstime / Caoerlei p9(td), Dreamstime / Monica Boorboor p9(te), Dreamstime / Mindauga Dulinska p9(ba), Dreamstime / Craig Russell p9(bb), p9(bc), p9(bd), p9(be), Dreamstime / Hugo Milne-Home p9(bf), Dreamstime / Yelena Panyukova p10(a), Dreamstime / Jiri Novotny p10(b), Dreamstime / Timurd p10(c), Dreamstime / Nilabarathi p10(e), Dreamstime / Oleksandr Delyk p10(f), Dreamstime / Andrii Kucher p10 (bag), Dreamstime / Vladimir Blinov p10(1), Dreamstime / Radub85 / p10(2), Dreamstime / Les Cunliffe p10(4), Dreamstime / Dstaerk p10(5), Dreamstime / Igor Terekhov p10 (backpack), Dreamstime / Vadim Ginzburg p10(6), Dreamstime / Konstantin Tavrov p10(8), Dreamstime / Tashka2000 p10(9), Dreamstime / Chimpinski p10(10), Dreamstime / Denis Babenko p11(b), Dreamstime / Slava296 p11(c), p11(d), Dreamstime / Natis76 p13(t1), Dreamstime / Mousemd p13(t2), Dreamstime/ Adina Nani p13(t3), Dreamstime / Anutik45 p13(t4), Dreamstime / Ingrid Prats p13(t5), Dreamstime / Mpfphotography p13(t6), Dreamstime/ Alancotton p13(t7), Dreamstime/ Alexlmx p13(t9), Dreamstime / Ericlefrancais p13(t12), Dreamstime / Krischam p13(t13), Dreamstime / Antonio Guillem p14(a), Dreamstime / Petro p14(e), Dreamstime / Vadymvdrobot p14(f), Kiosea39 p15(tb), p15(td), Dreamstime / Oocoskun p15(tc), Dreamstime / Zhukovsky p15(ba), Dreamstime / Jovan Barajevac p15(bb), Dreamstime / Dmitry Kalinovsky p15(bd), Dreamstime / Hongqi Zhang (aka Michael Zhang) p15(be), Dreamstime / Mauricio Jordan De Souza Coelho p15(bf), Dreamstime / Diana Eller p16, Dreamstime / Starstock p17(a), Dreamstime / Cmeree p19(1), Dreamstime / Viktorijareut p19(2), Dreamstime / Bahtiar Maulana p19(3), Dreamstime / Eleonora Ivanova p19(4), Dreamstime / Sergey Siz`kov p19(5), Dreamstime / Mark Vorobev p19(6), Dreamstime / Oxana Reshetnyova p19(7), Dreamstime / Vector Moon p19(8), Dreamstime / Julioaldana p19(9), Dreamstime / Segura Roser p19(10), Dreamstime / Mawielobob p19(11), Dreamstime / Marnikus p19(12), Dreamstime / Slava182 p19(13), Dreamstime / Mtlapcevic p19(14), Dreamstime / Artofphoto p20(bl), Dreamstime / Mimagephotography p20(trc), Dreamstime / Romrodinka p20(tr), Dreamstime / Nyul p20(brc), Dreamstime / Migfoto p20(br), Dreamstime / Nejron p21(a), Dreamstime / Wavebreakmedia Ltd p21(c), Dreamstime / Alberto Jorrin Rodriguez p22 (Phil), Dreamstime / Javiindy p22 (Kesha), Dreamstime / Imagecollect p24(tb), Dreamstime / Jenta Wong p24(td), Dreamstime / Savannah1969 p24(ba), Dreamstime / Tonyv3112 p24(bc), Dreamstime / Anastasiia Bobko p25(1), Dreamstime / Microvone p25(2), Dreamstime / Angelinnap25(4), Dreamstime / Artisticco Llc p25(5), Dreamstime / Ildar Galeev p26(6), Dreamstime / Andrei Krauchuk p26(7), Dreamstime / Dannyphoto80 p26(8), Dreamstime / Mast3r p26(9), Dreamstime / Blueringmedia p26(10), Dreamstime / Dmitry Rogatnev / p26(11), Dreamstime / Andrei Krauchuk p26(12), Dreamstime / Pdtnc p26t, Dreamstime / Gemenacom p26b, Dreamstime / Steve Allen p27 (Mexico), p27 (Brazil), p27 (Spain), p27 (Germany), p27 (Italy), p27 (Japan), Dreamstime / Denisismagilov p27 (China), Dreamstime / Sam74100 p28(a), Dreamstime / Sharplaninac p28(c), Dreamstime / Martinmark p29, Dreamstime / Kadettmann / p30(l), Dreamstime / Timaj p31, Dreamstime / Merggy p32 (spring), Dreamstime / Hubis p32 (summer), Dreamstime / Merggy p32 (fall), Dreamstime / Michael Sheehan p32 (winter), Dreamstime / Pavel Mastepanov p32(in), Dreamstime / Roman Sotola p32(on), Dreamstime / Jikung4u p32(at), Dreamstime / Wavebreakmedia Ltd p34(e), Dreamstime / Syda Productions p34(f), Dreamstime / Hclark5 p35(1), Dreamstime / Crazy80frog p35(2), Dreamstime / Marcio Silva p35(3), Dreamstime / Maglara p35(4), Dreamstime / Paul Topp p36(a), Dreamstime / Jonmilnes p36(b), Dreamstime / Kornilovdream p36(c), Dreamstime / Tomas Del Amo p36(e), Dreamstime / Telecast p36(f), Dreamstime / Dirima p36(g), Dreamstime / Sergeyzapotylok p36 (Pam), Dreamstime / Maxfx p36 (Steve), Dreamstime / Andrei Krauchuk p38(a), Dreamstime / LinaTruman p38(b), Dreamstime / Vector Moon p38(d), Dreamstime / Niek p39(b), Dreamstime / Loopall p40 (sun), Dreamstime / Topgeek p40 (wind), Dreamstime / Sommersby p40 (cloud), Dreamstime / Amiragee p40 (rain), Dreamstime / Jov43 p40 (snow), Dreamstime / Stas11 p40 (flog), Dreamstime / Ocusfocus p42(tl), Dreamstime / Kurhan p42(tc), Dreamstime / Johan Larson p42(tr), Dreamstime / Mauricio Jordan De Souza Coelho p42(bl), Dreamstime / Eldar Nurkovic p42(bc), Dreamstime / Johan Larson p42(br), Dreamstime / Roman Stetsyk p45, Dreamstime / Andrii Symonenko p47(1), (5), Dreamstime / Merggy p47(2), Dreamstime / Taily_sindariel p47(3), Dreamstime / Blueringmedia p47(4), Dreamstime / Klara Viskova p47(6), Dreamstime / Yusa48 p47(7), Dreamstime / Tmarchev p47(8), Dreamstime / Monkey Business Images p48(a), Dreamstime / Stephen Coburn p48(b), Dreamstime / Mariia Demydova p48(c), Dreamstime / Boggy p48(d), Dreamstime / Andrei Rahalski p48(e), Dreamstime / Antoniodiaz p48(br), Dreamstime / Starstock p50(tc), Dreamstime / Featureflash p50(tr), Dreamstime / Matt Antonino p51(t), Dreamstime / Lunamarina p51(br), Dreamstime / Scorpion26 p52(b2), Dreamstime / Andrei Krauchuk p53, Dreamstime / Michał Rojek p54 (ipad), Dreamstime / Yusakprahadi p55(b), Dreamstime / Naddiya p55(c), Dreamstime / Wolfberry p55(d), Dreamstime / Willeecole p55(e), Dreamstime / Oleg Tokarev p55(f), Dreamstime / Monkey Business Images p55(br), Dreamstime / Ylivdesign p57(A1), Dreamstime / Natee Srisuk p57(A2), Dreamstime / Applee p57(A3), Dreamstime / Liimon1303 p57(A4), Dreamstime / Gpgroup p57(A5), Dreamstime / Roberto Giovannini p57(A6), Dreamstime / Roberto Giovannini p57(A7), Dreamstiime / Vector p57(A9), Dreamstime / Yusakprahadi p57(B1), Dreamstime / Dennis Cox p57(B2), Dreamstime / Sabelskaya p57(B3), Dreamstime / Chris Eltringham p57(B4), Dreamstime / Mariya Khramtseva p57(B5), Dreamstime / Lemonadeserenade p57(B6), Dreamstime / Yusakprahadi p57(B7), Dreamstime / Lemonadeserenade p57(B8), Dreamstime / Artem Malyshko p57(C1), Dreamstime / Blueringmedia p57(C2), Dreamstime / Aleksangel p57(C3), Dreamstime / Natis76 p57(C4), Dreamstime / Amin11mario p57(C5), Dreamstime / Klara Viskova p57(C6), Dreamstime / Selvam Raghupathy p57(D1), Dreamstime / Leen Savoyar p57(D2), Dreamstime / Oleg Tokarev p57(D3), Dreamstime / Larryrains p57(D4), Dreamstime / Diamondimages p57(D5), Dreamstime / Yusakprahadi p57(D6), Dreamstime / Jackie Egginton p57(b2), Dreamstime / Julia Pfeifer p57(b4), Dreamstime / Hlaura p57(b6), Dreamstime / Tatianatatiana p58(br), Dreamstime / Wavebreakmedia Ltd p59, Dreamstime / Viorel Dudau p60(1), Dreamstime / Gregory Audureau p61(a), Dreamstime / Stephan Bock p61(b), Dreamstime / Ensuper p61(c), Dreamstime / Rodrusoleg p61(d), Dreamstime / Eti Swinford p61(e), Dreamstime / Nomadsoul1 p61(g), Dreamstime / Louella38 p61(h), Dreamstime / Saphire Ovadia p61 (sign), Dreamstime / Monkey Business Images p62(a), Dreamstime / Stephanie Frey p62(b), Dreamstime / Tanatat p62 (phone), Dreamstime / Servickuz p65(tl), Dreamstime / Artofphoto p65(tc), Dreamstime / Ocusfocus p65(tr), Dreamstime / Anthony Maragou p65(br), Dreamstime / Studio Dream p67(t), Dreamstime / Vadymvdrobot p67(a), Dreamstime / Kiosea39 p67(c), Dreamstime / Dmitry Kalinovsky p68(cc), Dreamstime / Bert Folsom p70(a), Dreamstime / Marazem p70(b), Dreamstime / Udra11 p70(c), Dreamstime / Alexander Tolstykh p70(e), Dreamstime / Denlarkin p70(f), Dreamstime / Duncan Noakes p70(g), Dreamstime / Sergii Kolesnyk p70(h), Dreamstime / Robert Kneschke p71(c), Dreamstime / Dmytro Konstantynov p71(d), Dreamstime / Monkey Business Images p71(f), Dreamstime / Elena Elisseeva p72 (Inamo), Dreamstime / Erin Cadigan p72 (Luigi's), Dreamstime / Monkey Business Images p72(b), Dreamstime / Maryna Patzen p73(t), Dreamstime / Warrengoldswain p73(bl), Dreamstime / Ivan Mikhaylov p73(bcl), Dreamstime / Martinmark p73(bcr), Dreamstime / Pro777 p73(br), Dreamstime / Likefermat p75(t), Dreamstime / Kristenelise p75(a), Dreamstime / Josephthomas p75(b), Dreamstime / Christian Bertrand pp75(c), 76, Dreamstime / Andrey Burmakin p75(d), Dreamstime / Robert Byron p77(t), Dreamstime / Rafael Ben Ari p78(a), Dreamstime / Ganeshkumar Durai p78(b), Dreamstime / Tyler Olson p78(c), Dreamstime / Dan Grytsku p80 (Brad), Dreamstime / Tupungato p80(bcl), Dreamstime / Alana Colbert p80(bcr), Dreamstime / Nikolai Sorokin p80(br), Dreamstime / Monkey Business Images p81(2), Dreamstime / Filipe Frazao p82(t), Dreamstime / Danflcreativo p82(b), Dreamstime / Mirko Vitali p83, Dreamstime / Mjak / p85(1), Dreamstime / Leen Savoyar p85(2), Dreamstime / Coliap / p85(3), Dreamstime / Dannyphoto80 p85(4), Dreamstime / Oleksii Koval p85(5), Dreamstime / Andegraund548 p85(6), Dreamstime / Elena Medvedeva p85(7), Dreamstime / Dmstudio p85(8), Dreamstime / Addictivex p85(9), Dreamstime / Pichayasri p85(10), Dreamstime / Neizu03 p85(11), Dreamstime / Viktorijareut p85(12), Dreamstime / Dmitriy Osminskiy p85(13), Dreamstime / Larisa Vasilyeva p85(14), Dreamstime / Marcio Goldzweig p85(15), Dreamstime / Lakhesis p89(3), Dreamstime / Lunamarina p89(4), Dreamstime / Pkazmierczak p89(2), Dreamstime / Pisit Rapitpunt p89(1), Dreamstime / Jorgenmac p90, Dreamstime / Burlesck p91(1), Dreamstime / Dannyphoto80 p91(2), Dreamstime / Barmaleeva p91(3), Dreamstime / Barbaliss p91(4), Dreamstime / Darja Tokranova p91(5), Dreamstime / Oceloti p91(6), Dreamstime / Dannyphoto80 p91(7), Dreamstime / Benchart p91(8), Dreamstime / Eknarin Maphichai p91(9), Dreamstime / Dannyphoto80 p91(10), Dreamstime / Kulikoks p91(11), Dreamstime / Martin Malchev p91(12), Dreamstime / Nyker1 p92(tl), Dreamstime / Darya Petrenko p92(cr), Dreamstime / Oblong1 p92(cl), Dreamstime / Feverpitched p92(br), Dreamstime / Volodymyr Ivash p95(cl), Dreamstime / Izf p95(cr), Dreamstime / Viorel Dudau p95(bl), Dreamstime / Darren Baker p95(br), Dreamstime / Ocusfocus pp96(a), 104(a), Dreamstime / Thuatha22 pp96(b), 104(b), Dreamstime / Photographerlondon pp96(c), 104(c), Dreamstime / Aleksandr Markin pp96(d), 104(d), Dreamstime / Artur Ilchishin pp96(e), 104(e), Dreamstime / Artofphoto pp96(f), 104(f), Dreamstime / Leo Bruce Hempell p109, Dreamstime / Vivian Seefeld p110, Dreamstime / Darrinhenry p113(t), Dreamstime / Ioana Grecu p113(b), Dreamstime / Pixelrobot p115 (pizza), Dreamstime / Laboko p115 (detergent), Dreamstime / Ilfede p115 (magazine), Dreamstime / Meghadesai p115 (DVD); **Getty Images** / NT Photography p9(tb), Getty / Massimo Merlin p9(tc), Getty / Sean Gallup / Staff p9(tf), Getty / Christopher Lee - FIFA / Contributor p9(tg), Getty / John Gress / Stringer p10(3), Getty / Scott Wintrow / Stringer p10(7), Getty / LEONELLO CALVETTI p10(d), Getty / Spaces Images p11(a), Getty / Trinette Reed p11(e), Getty / Richard I'Anson p11(f), Getty / Hill Street Studios p12(b), Getty / LEONELLO CALVETTI p13(t8), Getty / JoeLena p13(t10), Getty / rambo182 p13(t11), Getty / Blend Images - KidStock p15(ta), Getty / Justin Sullivan / Staff p15(bc), Getty / Mike Kemp p15(bg), Getty / Morsa Images (bh), Getty / Neustockimages p14(b), Getty / pkline p14(c), Getty / JGI/Jamie Grill p14(d), Getty / Jeff Kravitz / Contributor p17(b), Getty / Kevin Mazur / Contributor p17(c), Getty / PeopleImages p18 (Rosie), Getty / sturti p18 (Mike), Getty / Jose Luis Pelaez Inc.. p18 (Freda), Getty / John Holcroft p19(15), Getty / Westend61 p20(tl), Getty / Guido Mieth p20(tlc), Getty / andresr p20(blc), Getty / Rob Foldy / Contributor p21(b), Getty / SensorSpot p23, Getty / Pier Marco Tacca / Contributor p24(ta), Getty / David Wolff - Patrick / Contributor p24(tc), Getty / Ron Levine p24(bb), Getty / yuoak p25(3), Getty / Kutay Tanir p27 (USA), Getty / Mireya Acierto p28(t), Getty / Paper Boat Creative p28(b), Getty / Gaudilab p30(r), Getty / Ben Hider / Contributor p33(a), Getty / Trungdbnguyen p33(b), Getty / Simon Greenwood p33(c), Getty / levers2007 p33(br), Getty / Westend61 p34(a), Getty / Juice Images p34(b), Getty / Sam Edwards p34(c), Getty / STOCK4B-RF p34(d), Getty / Guido Cavallini p36(d), Getty / Bloomberg / Contributor p37 (logo), Getty / Bloomberg / Contributor p37(c), Getty / Miquel Benitez / Stringer p37(b), Getty / P2007 p38(c), Getty / Jens Magnusson p38(e), Getty / Kjell Linder p39(t), Getty / Baerbel Schmidt / p40(b), Getty / Ezra Bailey p46(b), Getty / Bryan Bedder / Staff p43, Getty / GAB Archive / Contributor p44(l), Getty / Ethan Miller / Staff p44(r), Getty / Stockbyte p48(f), Getty / Shirlaine Forrest / Contributor p50(tl), Getty / Dave Hogan / Contributor p50(b), Getty / Raphael Dias / Stringer p51(c), Getty / DEA / L. ROMANO / Contributor p51(bl), Getty / Ron Vesely / Stringer p51(bc), Getty / Brian Macdonald p54 (background), Getty / asiseeit / p58(tl), Getty / Bloomberg / Contributor p60(2), Getty / Dan Callister / Online USA p60(3), Getty / Rafael Ben Ari p60(4), Getty / mfto p61(f), Getty / Tony Barson p64(1), Getty / Kevin Mazur / Contributor p64(2), Getty / Jeff Vespa / Contributor p64(3), Getty / Kevin Mazur/Billboard Awards 2014 / Contributor p64(4), Getty / Johnny Nunez / Contributor p66(t), Getty / Plume Creative p67(b), Getty / PeopleImages p68(ca), Getty / PeopleImages p68(cb), Getty / Jamie Grill p70(d), Getty / Sergii Kolesnyk p71(a), Getty / Betsie Van Der Meer p71(b), Getty / Led p71(e), Getty / Thomas Barwick p72 (Steak shop), Getty / Monica Schipper / Contributor p75(e), Getty / CBS Photo Archive / Contributor p77(b), Getty / VCG / Contributor p78(d), Getty / Candybox Images p78(e), Getty / Yuri_Arcurs p80 (Steve), Getty / PeopleImages p80 (Rachel), Getty / xPACIFICA p80(bl), Getty / David Santiago Garcia p81(1), Getty / quavondo p81(3), Getty / Mats Silvan / Design Pics p81(4), Getty / Miquel Benitez / Contributor p81(4), Getty / Chris Parker p81(5), Getty / Westend61 p81(6), Getty / Amanda Hall / robertharding p84(b), Getty / Westend61 p86(t), Getty / STUDIO BOX p86(b), Getty / Hinterhaus Productions p87, Getty / Adrian Murrell / Staff p88(t), Getty / Adrian Murrell / Staff p88(b), Getty / Jennifer Robbins p89(b), Getty / Yuri_Arcurs p92(tr), Getty / Westend61 p92(bl), Getty / Brian Ach / Contributor p93, Getty / Dan Kitwood / Staff p94, Getty / Santi Visalli / Contributor p95, Getty / Bloomberg / Contributor p115 (shampoo), Getty / Tim Graham / Contributor p115 (wine); **Maximilian Stock Ltd.** p52.

CANIEM No. 2275

Macmillan Publishers S.A. de C.V. Insurgentes Sur 1886
Col. Florida, CP 01030
Álvaro Obregón
Ciudad de México
Tel: +52 (55) 5482 2200
elt@grupomacmillan.com

www.grupomacmillan.com www.macmillan.com.mx www.macmillanenglish.com



Impresso no Brasil,EGB,07 2024.